Reflections of a Queensland Country Girl

Cynthia Lindenmayer

This book is copyright. Apart from any fair dealing for the purpose of private study, research, criticism or review, as permitted under the Copyright Act, no part may be reproduced by any process without written permission. Enquiries should be addressed to the Publishers.

All rights reserved.

Third Edition 2012

National Library of Australia Cataloguing-in-Publication entry: (pbk)

Author: Lindenmayer, Cynthia.

Title: Reflections of a Queensland Country Girl / Cynthia Lindenmayer.

ISBN: 9781921920400 (pbk.)

Subjects: Lindenmayer, Cynthia.

Women--Queensland--Biography.

Queensland--Biography.

Dewey Number: 994.32

Typeset in Times New Roman 12pt

Published by Boolarong Press, Salisbury, Brisbane, Australia.

Printed and bound by Watson Ferguson & Company, Salisbury, Brisbane, Australia.

Acknowledgements

I wish to acknowledge the invaluable contribution made to the preparation of this work by Mrs Lesley Kopp, my husband's former loyal and over-worked secretary, who typed, re-typed, printed and collated the manuscript for the first edition, through numerous drafts, all in her precious spare time. I also acknowledge the efforts of my husband, Travis, as my editor and collaborator, who also typed the additional chapters for the second, and this third edition, as well as the Epilogue. Without their efforts, this would remain a collection of my own mostly illegible scribblings.

Contents

Time, the Enemy

I awake in the early hours of the morning, which is not an unusual thing. It's always a lonely feeling, like standing in a desert alone with nothing but white sand as far as you can see. Suddenly the security light flashes on and it's like a bright sun highlighting the desert. But it also brings you back to the reality that you're in bed alone, and it starts up the thoughts in your head like a generator. The usual night noises of the house are magnified, and you lie awake too scared to move. If you do you're sure the monster creatures which inhabit the night will come out of hiding and gobble you up. The security light goes off, and you start to relax, only to be awakened by the generator, that starts up your thoughts again.

You think of your past as a young girl and it seems that she is now a stranger to you. Your life seems to streak by like a flash of lighting through a dark sky.

My thoughts are now with my father. I see him in our rented fibro house, sitting at the head of the long wooden table, with the long stools where the family sat for the Sunday lunch, which was always the main meal of the week. It consisted of a big roast, with vegetables, gravy, and a pudding of some kind. The front door was always open in case someone called in, which they nearly always did. If no one called, you wondered why. What dreadful thing had befallen them? When someone did come, they would call through the open door: "Yoo hoo, anyone home?" Either mother or father would reply: "We are just having lunch, come and join us."

Then father's stories would start. They were mostly about "the great depression" (which left a lasting impression on him!), or about his loneliness as a young child on the bullock tracks with his father. He would tell how the noises of the curlews at night added to his loneliness, and his longing for the warmth of his mother's arms. He would say, "You lot don't know how easy you have it today. I wish I was born 30 years later, and had it so good." He would go on: "I remember how my mother drove a horse and sulky on the long, lonely road from Silverspur to Stanthorpe to have her fifth child. She took the two eldest girls with her and left my baby brother, Roy, aged ten months and myself, aged about five with father on the farm. He was a tough man, (not soft like me), who didn't talk much, only to chastise us. Night after night I would lie awake wishing I was with my mother, enjoying the softness of her embrace, instead of feeling the lash of father's tongue. While she was away he decided to take his team of horses (along with my brother and me) with a load of timber to the sawmill at Yarraman. At the snails pace of 14 miles a day, it meant weeks on the road. It was my job to ride Trixie, my pony, and drive the spare horses, while Roy lay on a dusty blanket in a tiny clearing in the centre of the horse-drawn table top wagon, surrounded by bales of hay and covered by a tarpaulin. I was just five! Without a word of a lie. I would like to see any of you do that today. My God, you don't know how easy you have it."

I now see him an 88 year old man with dementia sitting at another table at the old folks home all alone staring with a vacant look on his face. Mother and I approach this lonely old man to greet him. He has a startled look in his eyes, as if we are strangers. Every now and then there is a flicker of recognition in his eyes, which reminds us of how he once was but then the flame goes out as though a cap had been placed over a candle flame to extinguish it. Once again he is gone from us.

I drive past where our house used to be. It is now a cluster of shops. Memories flood in. I see my little black and white Foxy dog "Soda" and the movie star posters plastered all over the bedroom wall where I would lie for hours fantasising about how I would be discovered and become one of them. I would try to roll my hair like Betty Hutton, sprawl on the bed, call Soda to jump up with me, and lie with one arm around him and my foot on the wall where the posters were. I would say to Soda: "One day I'll be a famous movie star and you'll be my famous dog and you'll have a diamond studded collar". I would then hear heavy footsteps, and quickly push Soda off the bed as father appeared in the door-way, growling: "Is that dog on the bed?" I would reply: "Nooooo Dad". "Well he shouldn't even be in the house", he would reply, as he walked away. The minute he was gone, I would pat the bed and Soda would jump back up again to join me.

The soft mattress on the bed had a large ridge down the middle which my sister and I (who shared the bed) had put there to make sure we each stayed on our side. We each made threats to the other about what would happen if we crossed the line which we would do at our own risk. Occasionally the line would be crossed and there would be an awful scuffle, with the mattress, my sister and I all landing with a thud on the floor to be greeted by Soda barking and skidding across the lino. Then dad would yell out: "What's going on in there", to which each of us would reply: "She was on my side." Dad would then threaten to bring the dreaded strap to sort us out, while mother would cry out: "I never thought I would rear such daughters." Later on, when my sister was making plans to get married, at night in bed I would lie there thinking: "I can't wait. It will be great to have this bed to myself." In making that wish I was forgetting the times when family and friends would sit around the kitchen table with their cups of tea discussing the latest outrage (like the prisoners' escape from jail) and later that night my sister and I would flatten the ridge and huddle together when one would say, "Shh! What's that noise?" When at last she got married I couldn't believe how much I missed her and how lonely I felt in that bed on my own, as I am now, 45 years later.

I drag myself out of bed to make a cup of Chamomile tea to help me sleep. As I get back into bed with my cup of tea I look at the tea bag and remember my mum standing at the old wood stove with the fire iron in her hand, stirring the embers of the dying fire. The old black kettle is standing on top of the stove with steam coming from the narrow spout and its lid popping up and down. I think that tea doesn't taste as good now as it did then, or is it just nostalgia for the cuppa which was the magic brew for all our troubles?

I now see my mother seated at the wooden table in the kitchen with the cup of strong black tea, which she always drank, in front of her. It is night-time, and she is sewing by hand by the light of a kerosene lamp which sits in the middle of the table casting flickering shadows into the dim corners of the room. She has a well worn thimble on the index finger of her left hand, and I marvel at the quickness of her beautiful slender hands as she skilfully stitches up the hem of the frock she is just completing. As she sews, she tells my sister and me of her one great regret in life. When she was a young girl working as a waitress in a country hotel, a city man and his wife, who were passing through town, commented upon the lovely dresses she wore and asked where she got them. She replied that she designed and made them herself, as she did, all her clothes. The couple were very impressed, and offered to take her to the city to work for them as a designer of women's clothing. Her excitement at the prospect was soon dashed by her father, who would not hear of her going. To him, city folks were like aliens from a distant planet who would "definitely be up to no good and were not to be trusted".

My mother was a striking woman with her jet black hair and her fabulous figure. She was always dressed in the latest fashion and I was constantly in awe of her beauty. As I think of her I see this frail lady of 87 years, slow of movement, but with a smile that lights up her face and brings back her youthfulness in a flash.

I think of the last time I saw her visiting dad at the old folks home, desperately trying to bring him back as he once was. But it's not to be. That young man has gone forever. She walks out with defeat in her eyes and her shoulders slumped. With tears streaming down her face she says: "I never thought it would end up like this!"

Now I am back in the old fibro house. Mum is demanding: "Who shut the front door?" No one answers. We all know it is to be left open to let the breeze in and so that her friends, Mackie and Dorrie, will know she is home and drop in for a cuppa and the local gossip. How things have changed. Now this frail old lady with the frightened look in her eyes is always asking: "Is the front door locked and bolted and the windows too? You never know who's around these days."

When Mackie and Dorrie did drop in, they would sit with mum at the wooden table in the kitchen, and say in an apprehensive way, things like: "Did you see the strange clouds this morning? Have you ever seen clouds like that?" Dorrie would say as she fanned herself with her hand: "It's getting hotter every year. Bill (Dorrie's husband) says 'It's all to do with the atom bomb and it'll be the end of the world soon, you mark my words'". My sister and I, having overheard this conversation, would peer at the clouds from our window that night and repeat: "Bill Jones reckons the end of the world is coming soon, and it's all due to the atom bomb". Now, 45 years later, it is pollution and the breakdown of the ozone layer, or a collision with a comet that we fear will bring the world to an end.

Next thing I am riding in the car. I see a young girl standing in the shop where our house used to be. She has long thick black hair that reminds me of my sister. I think of her standing in the kitchen of our house where <u>everything</u> happened! She is looking nervous, asking dad can she go to the pictures with a boy she just met. Father has a stern face and says: "On the condition that I meet the boy first and you don't let him buy your ticket, because then you would be under an obligation to him."

At that time, when she was just discovering boys, our mother and father had different ways of dealing with the fear of an unwanted pregnancy and the shame which would accompany it. Father's strategy was to ensure that she was never alone with a boy for long enough for that to happen. If a boy visited, she had to stay in the fully lit lounge room and, to her embarrassment, father would call out in a stern voice, every 5 minutes: "It's time you got to bed". That was enough to make any boy bolt after a few calls. If she went out with a boy, I had to trail along with her as a chaperone.

Mother's strategy, on the other hand, was to tell her to be careful if any boys tried to kiss her because their "big thing" would expand and form a bulge in their pants, and if it touched her a "germ" would jump across onto her and make her pregnant. Having heard (and believed) that story, when arriving home with my sister and her boyfriend, I would precede them into the yard, and wait anxiously in the shadow of the house while she said good-night to him. If I saw him kiss her, I would call out "If you don't hurry up, I'll tell dad". She still complains, 45 years later, about my spying on her, but she doesn't seem to realize I only did it when I saw her get too close to the "bulge" in the boys pants and I was trying to prevent her from getting pregnant!

These are my memories. Then I think of how dad loved to tell his stories over the years, but his memories are now lost forever.

When we are with him in the old folks home I can see the one thing he hasn't lost is his principles. His leg is aching and he keeps touching it. The nurse brings a cushion to ease his pain. Father puts his old crippled hand in his pocket in search of money, and with a worried look on his face whispers: "I haven't got any money." We laugh sadly and say: "You don't have to pay dad." His principles are engraved on his mind and will die with him.

I feel like screaming: "I want my parents back as they used to be." I want the conflict and all. I want to see mum getting dressed for the races as I lie on the bed watching her and she says: "I'm going to win and bring home the big money today, and I will buy you whatever you want!" I want dad back writing the book about his life although he drove us mad doing it and we whispered to each other: "Not that story again." But mum and dad are slipping away just as the soapy glass slipped out of my hand and shattered to pieces on the tiled floor this morning. Just as there was nothing I could do to put the broken pieces together, so I cannot stop time (the enemy) ticking away.

I think of my children struggling with their lives as young adults. Life is like a relay race. You start out with such gusto to reach the end, but as you slow down puffing and staggering you hand the baton on to the next generation, and they do the same. Sometimes the baton slips out of your hand, as respect for others and honesty fall, but if you hold the baton tightly enough and don't let your values slip, then time isn't wasted.

My thoughts are interrupted by a ringing. It takes me a few seconds to realise it's the alarm. I look over to the clock ticking by. It's time (the enemy) to rise and start another day.

The 'illegal' structure of the Battle of Biloela.

Tom and Cetress, circa 1950's.

Homestead in Taroom area.

The caravan in which Tom and Cetress travelled around selling and cutting hair etc.

The overland 'Beauty Salon' in the main street of Theodore.

Cynthia at age 15.

Dunny Business

The day has ended, and I am back in my bed again. Once more I have awakened in the early hours. Was that a noise I heard? I put on the bedside light and start writing down my thoughts, propped up on pillows. That seems to drive the night creatures back into their hiding places, and my fear subsides. I fantasise that my scribblings will one day make a great play or movie. That makes me realize that I still have fantasies. I wonder if other grown up people do too? My father certainly did.

I remember him telling us, whilst seated at the kitchen table, how once he thought his fantasy of becoming a rich man had come true when, as a young lad, he was offered a great job which paid 5 pounds 12 shillings and 6 pence a week. He heard it was "a government job", but when he turned up to start he was told: "It's not the sweetest job mate, but the pay's good, and you'll learn what all your neighbours have in their guts. It's the sanitary man!" Although that dampened his fantasy a little, he could still see the money sign in front of the sanitary cart, and saw it as a stepping stone to his own business one day. So he took it on.

He went on to tell how one day, after work (and a good hot bath!) as he walked along the street with his hair slicked down with Californian Poppy hairoil, feeling the warmth of his new found wealth, he ran into a mate who was with his girlfriend. She had a girlfriend with her, to whom she introduced him. Although he was fairly shy, he was quite proud of the fact that he was able to keep up a conversation with her.

He told her he had "a government job" and arranged a date with her for the next evening. As he walked away, he puffed out his chest, patted himself on the back, and said to himself: "Well, I surely impressed that sweet young thing. She'll never guess my 'government job' is as the man who comes around".

Next day, as he went about his work, Dad was high with his fantasies about his sweetie. He whistled as he carried a full sanitary can on his shoulder towards the cart. Suddenly, he pulled up short, and found himself face to face with the sweet young girl. He got such a fright, he jumped and dropped the can right at her feet. The lid popped off, the contents splashed, and the sweet young thing was left not smelling so sweet, while he bolted. He was so embarrassed, he just wanted to die. But he told us: "Remember, no one really dies from embarrassment, and some of those embarrassing moments which we all experience will be tomorrow's funny stories".

Sitting up in bed reminds me of how I used to tell bedtime stories to my two children, one lying on each side of me before going to their own beds to sleep. One story had a reference to a backyard toilet. "What's a backyard toilet Mum?" they asked. "Well" I said "it's a little house well back from the big house where we would do our number ones and our number twos in a black can which was under a wooden seat with a hole in it, a bit like the WC you sit on. Hanging on the side wall by a piece of string attached to a nail, would be pieces of cut up newspaper, which we used to clean ourselves (except for the newsprint left on out bottoms), and beside the seat was a box full of sawdust, with an empty jam tin which we used to sprinkle sawdust over the business so it wouldn't smell so much and to keep away the flies. Once a week the sanitary man would come around and change the can. He would take out the full one, put a lid on it, slip an empty one in it's place, and then heave the full one up onto his shoulder and run with it to his truck waiting in the street. You could smell the truck coming two blocks away!" "Oh yuk!" one of the children said.

That led me to tell them the story of how, as a young girl in a country town I went one day to play with the daughter of the matron at the hospital. After a while, I said to my friend "I've got to go to the lav", and headed out the back door. "Where are you going?", she said. "To the dunny", I replied. "It's not out there", she said. "It's in here", and she took me to a door off the hallway. As I entered the little room, I said to myself: "Gee, fancy having the dunny inside the house!" As I sat on the seat, I saw this chain hanging down, and wondered what it was. Out of curiosity, I pulled it. My god. Water rushed up from beneath me and hit my bottom, and just kept running. I jumped up, and ran home as fast as I could, where I hid under my bed, sure that by now the hospital would be flooded out. Any moment I expected the police to come and take me away, for my crime.

My children chuckled at my stupidity, which made me think how life repeats itself because my sister and I had chuckled in just the same way over my Dad's story about his escapade as a sanitary man.

Recalling my apprehension about the police barging through the front door reminds me of how, a few days later, father bowled in through the door full of excitement, just as Mum was getting our Saturday lunch ready. He was the local barber, and I can still see him in his white shirt with the black bow-tie, and his white lap-over coat with a comb sticking up out of the top pocket. "Hurry up with the lunch, love" he said. "I've just seen an ad in the paper for a Wella Steam Hair Waving unit for sale at Baralaba, and I'd like to try and get over there to get it before someone else does. If we use out heads in more ways than one I'm sure there's money to be made with it."

After a hurried lunch and a phone call to the vendor of this unit, we all set off to Baralaba, in a borrowed car, to inspect this new-fangled gadget. I remember how Dad persuaded the vendor to give him and Mum a demonstration of the machine by asking: "How can I be sure it's in good working order?" The man proceeded to call his daughter into the room, sit her in a chair, and go through the complicated procedure of perming her hair while Mum and Dad watched. They carefully noted how each roller placed in the child's hair was interconnected with hoses, the exact amount of cotton wool placed between each roller to prevent scalding of the scalp, and how the drainage hose was connected and draped over the girl's shoulder into a dish on the floor whilst the feeder hose was connected from the first roller to the steam tank which was preheated by the firing of a primus stove. After the necessary time, the primus was switched off, the hoses disconnected, and each roller carefully removed. We were all amazed at how, after a quick brush, the young girl presented a head full of beautiful soft natural-looking curls. Dad was immediately sold, and proceeded to wrap up the deal as quickly as possible.

After we got the machine home, the first people Mum and Dad practised on were my sister and me. We felt quite smug with out newly permed hair, which was Dad's clever way of advertising the new process which was soon to be available (at a price) in Mum's newly-opened ladies' hairdressing salon beside Dad's barber shop.

There were two streets of shops in our town, and Mum's hairdressing salon was in the main street. It had a large front window which, as I look back on it, became my window on the world, just as the TV screen has become our window on a much bigger world today. I recall how, each morning as Mum opened her shop, I would draw her attention to the man who owned the shop opposite. He would stand in his doorway with his hands in his pockets and look, first one way, and then the other, along the street. As he did so, he would roll his testicles from side to side with his hands. It became our ritual, each morning, to watch this man going through his ritual of, as Mum called it, "playing pocket billiards". We always had a comment about him, and one I remember making was: "Hey Mum, if a woman did that they'd call her looney tunes, but for a man it's regarded as normal!"

When a customer came in for a hair perm, I would hand Mum the rollers and cotton wool, and listen to the gossip. Having a hair-do seemed to bring on an urge to tell their life story, or at least the latest episode. Mum often said she could make more money as a blackmailer than a hairdresser, but also warned me never to repeat anything I heard in the shop. "It's a good way to lose business. Silence is golden" she said.

Sometimes as I handed her the rollers, the customer's attention would turn to me. "Have you started a Glory Box yet, love?" one asked. "I was just telling her the other day its time to start" Mother replied. "I bought her a pair of towels to get her started." Flo (the customer) said:

"Yes, I didn't have to buy towels for years after I was married. They're great things, Glory Boxes, they can set you up for life."

When Mum was doing the late afternoon customers, I would think back to Flo's notion of being "set up for life" when, on looking out through my window on the world, I would see her, and others like her, sitting in their Holden utes outside the pub, waiting for their husbands. Their kids would be running around, jumping in and out of the cars, with their fish and chip dinners wrapped up in newspaper, or spilling the raspberry drink, which a father had so generously handed through the car window before dashing back into the bar for another round.

These women would have been up early to milk the cows, side by side with their husbands, then cook a hearty breakfast for the family, and do a heavy wash by hand, with only the copper boiler to help, before accompanying their husbands to town for the fortnightly shopping trip. It was on these trips that the women had the chance for an occasional hair-do, and a gossip, whilst their husbands looked forward to a few beers with their farming mates at the pub before heading home. Many a time I had seen one of these women, weary of waiting and tending the noisy children in the confines of the ute after such a long day, blow the horn to summon her husband from the bar only to have him emerge, and shout drunkenly: "Shut up you bitch, I'll come when I'm ready." I would turn to Mum and say: "Is that what I'm setting myself up for with my Glory Box?"

I recall how, years later, to my great delight, I saw (through my other window on the world – the TV set) how two daring women had chained themselves to the bar of the Regatta Hotel in Brisbane in protest at women being excluded from public bars. That was an early example of women's lib in operation, which has changed how men and women relate in ways those farmers and their wives would never have thought possible.

I now become aware of the faint scent of lavender from the sachet which I keep in my pillow case. That reminds me of sitting on the bed which I shared with my sister in the little fibro house, watching her going through her honeymoon lingerie from her Glory Box shortly before her wedding. As she picks up each delicate item she caresses it with her hand before dreamily brushing it against her check to feel the silkiness of it and to enjoy the faint smell of lavender from the scented soap which she had lovingly placed amongst these precious things. As I picture this I begin to snuggle down into the softness of my pillow and feel myself drifting off. The pen falls from my fingers, and I lazily reach across and switch off the light, surrendering to sleep.

Travis and Cynthia with the Travis's parents at a Ball in Biloela.

The Strength of a Mother's Love

Getting ready for bed tonight seems different. It's later than usual, as I have had my nephew visiting me. He has come to the city to attend a Real Estate Seminar. We sat up well into the night having a few glasses of wine, which made us quite talkative and reminiscent about the highs and lows of our family life. He has a child of his own now, which makes my parents great-grandparents! The relay of life goes on. I asked him: "What made you go into real estate?" He replied: "I was so impressed by your father's big car, when I was growing up, I decided to follow his footsteps into Real Estate. It seemed to be where the big money was to be made."

As I prepare for bed, I feel a lot more relaxed than usual having someone else in the house. Just as I slip between the sheets I pick up my pen to write, and immediately begin to think about the family discussions we used to have at the Sunday lunch table, where Dad's stories always held the floor.

One particular time comes to mind when one of our frequent visitors said to Dad: "Tom, I've noticed that you have a lot of trouble opening your hands, and I wonder why and how you ever managed to become a barber."

"There's quite a story to that, Jack" said Dad, "which you will be amazed to hear", and set about telling it.

I gave Mum a slight kick under the table, and we exchanged knowing looks. We had heard this story many times before. At that age

I didn't appreciate the suffering and striving behind it as I do now.

"I w's only 18 at the time" said Dad, "but I remember it as if it w's yesterdee. I w's as fit and as strong as a mallee bull in them days (which you had to be to handle them dunny cans without spilling 'em) and a pretty fair horseman too, even if I say so m'self. That day I'd ridden me Uncle Bill's horse in the picnic races at Euky, just outside Stanthorpe, and I'd booted him home a winner, so I w's pretty pleased with m'self. There w's to be a race ball that night in town, and at the end of the meeting Bill asked me to ride his horse the few miles back to his property and come back with his family in the sulky. Bill had to stay in town to organize the dance."

"It w's bloody near dark as I mounted up and headed for Bill's place. The horse was skittish from the start, and took fright at something immediately (God knows what). He pulled so hard, I had trouble holding him. The harder I tried to rein him in, the faster he went and with his head towards home I doubt there w's a rider alive who could've! Next thing the mongrel bolted off the road and ran headlong into a wire netting fence around an orchard. As he reared to free himself I lost the reins. As I tried to reach over his shoulder to gather th'm, the bastard galloped so close to a tree that me noggin hit the tree, smashing me skull and knocking me out of the saddle. Trouble was, as luck would have it, one of me feet w's caught up in the stirrup. The stupid bloody horse continued to bolt along the fence line dragging me behind, until he came to a fallen tree, which he proceeded to jump. M' free leg went under the tree, and the one caught in the stirrup followed the horse over it. Luckily the impact broke the stirrup leather, and the horse raced on towards home leaving me behind."

"I'm told it w's several hours before the search party, organized when I didn't turn up at the dance, found me, semi-conscious, covered in blood, and unable t' move. M' fists were tightly clenched, and stayed that way for a long time. When I woke up at last in the Stanthorpe hospital I found mother sitting beside me reading the Bible. I tried to talk to her, but all that came out was meaningless babble. I w's pretty damn scared then, I c'n tell y'. Mercifully I felt no pain at that stage. I thought that w's a blessing, and didn't realize how badly I w's hurt.

Only by overhearing some scraps of conversation between Mum and the doctor did I come to realize that I couldn't feel anything b'cause I w's partly paralysed, they feared permanently."

"To cut a long story short, they eventually gave up in the hospital and sent me home a bed-ridden cripple. They reck'nd I'd never walk again, but they didn't count on Mum's faith and persistence, and my sheer determination. With her constant care, encouragement, and prayers I was gradually able to regain some feeling and limited movement in m' arms and legs. Mum hit on the bright idea of making a four wheel trolley, which I c'ld lie across and push m'self around the house, with m' legs as they gradually got stronger. Bit by bit I w's able to use m' arms, too t' help me get about. But I still couldn't open m' hands, which remained tightly clenched. To help me overcome that, Mum gave me pencils and encouraged me to spend hours picking 'em up and dropping 'em again. I got sick of the look of those bloody pencils, I can tell you but they certainly helped a lot. As I began to master that, Mother gave me rubber balls to pick up and squeeze to strengthen my hands and arms. From that, I graduated to a push bike, from which I came many gutsers before I c'ld eventually ride it right 'round the yard unaided. By then (nearly three years after the accident) I was well on the way to recovery, but m' hands have never fully recovered and y've no doubt noticed I drag one leg when I walk."

"Yeah, Tom, that's fascinating" said Jack, "but you still haven't explained how you became a bloody barber!"

"I'm getting to that, Jack, hold your horses!" said Dad. "Although I was greatly improving, Mother c'ld see I'd never be fit for heavy manual work again (mind you, I've proved her wrong there more than once!) and she was very worried about m' future. I didn't have enough education for an office job, and there weren't many of them about anyway, in them days. At last we settled on barbering because no qualifications were needed and the work wasn't too hard (except for the bloody standing, which we didn't think about then!). But how was I to learn the trade and get some customers? Mother hit on an idea. It was a beauty. In them days it cost sixpence for a haircut, and she offered the parents of the local children a deal that w's too good to refuse. She said she'd pay them sixpence per child to let me cut their hair. So I began my barbering career in reverse, with no paying customers, but plenty of willing ones! I found it hard at the start, with me crippled hands, but with practice I soon got the hang of it and was eventually able to start charging m' customers. And that, Jack, is how I became a barber, and a bloody good'n too! But you'll be the first to know I've just clinched a deal to sell m' barbering business and go into real estate. That's where the big money is to be made, you mark my words!"

I marvel at my grandmother's foresight in getting Dad started in a trade which he could manage. She was a remarkable woman. She had seven children, and an incredibly hard life, but that's another story. In her later years, after her husband died and all her kids had grown up, she settled in Brisbane (the outskirts in those days, now a relatively close in suburb!) where we used to visit her from time to time.

Later, after I moved to Brisbane, and before I married my husband, I lived with her for a time. Even then, she was still very much a country woman, with the fowl run in the back yard from which she collected the eggs and sold a few to the local shop. In those days tradesmen like the butcher and baker still called at the door on their regular rounds. I can still see the occasion when she had some friends coming to visit and wanted to have fresh chicken for dinner. The baker arrived just as she had made up her mind to kill one of her fowls for the meal.

"Son, do me a favour and knock the head off one of them chooks, will you" she asked.

"OK. Mrs C" he said, "but I could go a nice cup-a-tea, and one of your lamingtons, afterwards. We can't match them at the bakery!"

"Right-y-oh" said grandma.

He proceeded to dispatch the chook in a flash, and soon had his feet under Grandma's kitchen table enjoying his cuppa.

"I needed that", he said "It's been a long day. I've been on the go since 3 o'clock this morning."

Now-a-days, as I pass through the supermarket and see the

hundreds of neatly dressed frozen chickens all lined up, I can't help thinking of grandma, and her chooks, and how she taught me the art of chicken plucking in her back yard at Carina.

"A lovely boy, that baker" she would say, after he had gone on his way. "Not like that butcher's boy, with his shifty eyes."

One day when he called with the meat supply that butcher's boy opened his shifty eyes so wide they stood out like butcher's blocks, when grandma opened the meat parcel, examined it with a critical eye, and said of one piece of steak: "I wouldn't eat that. It's only fit for a dog." So saying, she tossed the ragged looking piece to her dog Shep, who scarpered off with it in his mouth with tail wagging. From that day Shep always greeted the butcher's boy like a member of the family, and the butcher never sent grandma a second-class cut of meat again.

Later again, after I married my husband and lived permanently in Brisbane, we kept in touch with grandma through her declining years. I remember the sadness we all felt when Dad and his brother arranged her admission to a nursing home due to her increasing dementia and crippling arthritis. After that, whenever Dad came to Brisbane and visited her he would come home depressed and say: "I hate going there to see the Old Girl like that. I hope someone shoots me before I get to that stage." Mum would reply: "You'll be bloody lucky if we don't shoot you before you get to that stage", and laugh uproariously.

Dad's words come vividly back to mind now, when I visit Dad in the Old Folks home and see him looking for all the world like his mother did at the same age.

As these thoughts begin to make me sad, I glance across at the clock on my bedside table. It's well after midnight, and my eyes are feeling heavy. Tomorrow is another day. I allow my heavy eyes to close, and drift into dream-filled sleep.

Home-Grown Entertainment

Tonight, as I prepare for bed, I am thinking about the television programme I was watching earlier this evening. It was a very entertaining musical programme with much dancing and singing. It occurs to me that a great deal of our entertainment these days comes from passively watching television in our own homes, with little involvement of people outside our immediate families. That contrasts sharply with my youth when, with no television, we created our own entertainment much more than we do today.

I recall how my father, who was a born entrepreneur, was constantly dreaming up ideas for entertainment, not only of ourselves, but also of others, in our small hometown of Biloela. Some of those ideas were very successful, while others were not quite so.

One of his many brainwaves was to organise a "townies" versus "bushies" sporting competition, which was held at the town sportsground. Events arranged included buckjumping, log-sawing, three-legged races, catching a greasy pig, chaff-bag races and many more.

One particular event evoked much merriment and shenanigans amongst both the participants and the spectators. It involved married couples, or other male/female combinations, and required the male partner of each combination to wheel his female partner in a wheelbarrow over a measured course which encompassed much uneven ground. The bumps in the terrain to be traversed, coupled with the frantic efforts of each male partner to outdo his rivals, led to many of the female participants being unceremoniously tossed, sometimes several times, from their barrows, with consequential scrambling to regain their berths without incurring too much indignity, all urged on by their male partners and the raucous cheers of the delighted audience.

The whole contest was run progressively over several weekends, as some farmers and townies would be available on one weekend, but not the next. After each weekend of competition, the scores of the two teams would be tallied and the progress scores posted in various shop windows to maintain the intensity of the rivalry between town and country. Many a farmer or townie who had been unable or unwilling to participate at the start of the competition became drafted, through peer pressure, into subsequent rounds, in order to try to uphold the pride of his or her particular group.

Although the event began in a spirit of good-natured fun, which was maintained for a time, as the weeks passed the tone gradually changed to one of serious rivalry. People from one side or the other began to accuse their rivals of cheating, or the judges of bias in the selection of winners. Wars of words occasionally erupted, and some of these escalated into fisticuffs, particularly after some of the protagonists had downed a few beers.

I cannot now recall whether there was ultimately a winner proclaimed, and, if so, which group took out the honours. But, gradually it ground to a halt, and life returned more or less to normal.

Another of Dad's bright ideas was to try to organise a local greyhound racing competition. With that in mind, he called a public meeting in the local hall to put forward his proposal, which was warmly received by a sufficient number of citizens to make the idea appear viable. At Dad's suggestion, a number of residents agreed to acquire dogs for that purpose, and Dad undertook the task of approaching the local Council for permits, and doing other necessary spadework to get the idea up and running.

Dad, himself, acquired two greyhounds which he hoped to race. They were beautiful creatures, with very sleek coats, kind eyes and gentle dispositions. Dad delegated to me the task of walking his two dogs each morning, before I went to school. Every morning, at first light, I would set out, bare-footed, with my two charges on their leashes, for a long walk around the town's outskirts.

For a time I enjoyed these walks, as they took me past many of the town's older timber buildings, including a saddlery shop. I usually poked my head in there to say hello to the kindly saddler, with his leathery hands and face, who was also an early starter. I recall how he always had a stub of a roll-your-own cigarette dangling from his lower lip at the corner of his mouth, and I marvelled at his ability to talk without ever removing it. I also recall the warm and enticing smell of leather that always pervaded the shop. My walks also took me past the fences of some small farmlets adjacent to the town, where I might see one or two cows grazing, or being called in for milking.

Another feature of these walks that excited my interest was the occasional appearance, adjacent to my route, of a steam-drawn goods train. The slow, rattling passage of these lumbering beasts would mesmerise me, causing me to pause on my journey to watch their departure. To this day the sound of a passing train invokes in me strong nostalgic feelings.

All the pleasure and feelings that I have described arising from my early morning walks came to a sudden and unexpected end one morning as I neared my home. A stray cat suddenly emerged from behind a fence and crossed our path. My two dogs immediately succumbed to their natural instinct, and gave chase, baying for the poor cat's blood. I tried to hold them, and clung tightly to their leashes, only to be dragged bodily across the rough ground, badly skinning my knees and elbows, the pain forcing me to relinquish my hold on the leashes. To my horror, the released dogs quickly caught the unfortunate cat, and tore it to bloody pieces before my eyes. Shocked and distraught, and racked with uncontrollable sobs, I somehow managed to catch and regain control of the dogs, and dragged them home.

As I entered the house, still bawling my eyes out, Mum and Dad jumped out of bed to investigate, to be confronted by my mixture of anger, shock, pain and frustration.

"What's the matter?" yelled Mum, her eyes wide with fear.

"I'm never taking those dogs for a walk again!" I screamed, between sobs.

In response to Mum and Dad's anxious questions I stammered out an explanation for my state, and kept repeating, over and over, my determination never to walk "those rotten dogs" again. To my surprise, Dad made no attempt to argue with me, but both he and Mum tried to calm me whilst attending to my wounds, and explaining that it was just the nature of the dogs to chase small, furry, fast moving creatures. Although I eventually quietened, and went off to school with my wounds dressed, I was not happy. And I never did walk the dogs again.

For some reason of which I am unaware, the proposed dog racing never did eventuate. In due course, however, the town became home to an unusually large number of part greyhounds, which was the subject of comment by casual visitors to the town from time to time.

Not all of our entertainment in those days took place outside the home. Much of it simply involved gatherings of friends at the home of one or the other for a game of cards, or a sing-along, or just an exchange of stories. My Mum played the piano-accordion, by ear, and my Dad the spoons. Many a night passed noisily and happily to their accompaniment. On cold winter's nights we would sit around the old wood-fired stove in the kitchen, gossiping and nibbling away at such things as boiled and salted peanuts that Mum would have cooked up earlier in a big boiler on the stove, before spreading them out to dry and cool on the wire base of one of our old beds carried out into the yard for that purpose.

I remember one particular night when Mum and a couple of her female friends were sitting around the stove chatting, while Dad was preparing to go out to attend a meeting of the local branch of the Masonic Lodge. At that time, those meetings were held in the School of Arts hall. He had not long joined the Masons, which he did, he said, because he believed it would help him in his business, as a local barber. I was intrigued by his little ornamental apron, which I had seen laid out on the bed before he began to dress. I had heard talk about a secret handshake, but, try as I might, I could not entice Dad to disclose the nature of it, or anything else about what went on at their meetings.

Not long after Dad left that night, Mum said to me, "We're going out for a while, Cynth. We won't be too long." Then, after briefly opening and closing the oven door, she added, "Pull out the rice custard after about another five minutes."

She and her friends then left the house, whispering together in a conspiratorial way. I knew at once that Mum was up to some tomfoolery, because she always delighted in pranks and practical jokes. I soon forgot about that, as I played with my little dog, Soda, who loved chasing and retrieving a tennis ball which I would throw to various parts of the house.

Some time later Mum and her two friends hurried back into the house, looking flustered and out of breath. As they sat around the kitchen table, Mum brought out the brandy bottle. She always maintained that brandy was good for settling the nerves or an upset stomach. Although Dad frowned on women drinking, he did accept that "a drop of brandy" was acceptable occasionally for medicinal purposes only. As they sipped away at their brandy, I listened to their muffled talk, in the course of which Mum often put her hand up to her mouth and, with eyes wide, said things like, "Ooh, ah! What have we done? If Tom finds out it was us there'll be hell to pay." I believed that, because I had often heard him rouse at her over her practical jokes. "They'll get you into big trouble one day, you mark my words!" he frequently admonished her.

As I listened in to their talk I gradually learned what it was they had done. "Don't you breathe a word of this to anyone, Cynth," Mum urged, and to this day I have not done so. However, I think that sufficient time has now passed for me to tell the tale.

The three conspirators had sneaked down to the School of Arts, armed with a bundle of 'Tom-Thumb' firecrackers and a box of matches. They were aware that the hall had a gap in one of its side walls large enough to admit a small package. Under cover of darkness they tip-toed to the side of the hall near this hole, lit the fuse of the 'Tom-Thumb' bundle, and quickly pushed it through the hole into the hall. As the crackers began to explode noisily, in a staccato fashion like a machine gun being fired, they ran quickly down the laneway which separated the hall from the hotel, and took refuge in one of the staff rooms located at the rear of the hotel. They gained access to this hiding place by knocking loudly and calling out to the female occupant, whom they knew. There they sheltered, with the room in darkness, whilst a frantic search went on outside for the perpetrators of the recent outrage. They had been able to witness this by peering through a curtained window of the darkened room to see, first Masons, and later policemen, running about with torches in search of them. We later learned that the Masons had summoned the police from the public telephone situated outside the hall after they had regained their composure sufficiently from the initial shock of the noisy and unexpected interruption of their proceedings.

Later, when Dad returned home from the curtailed meeting, and found the three women sitting around the table drinking brandy, he first gave them a stern, disapproving look. However, on being told by Mum that they all had "upset tummies from something we ate", he soon joined them for a brandy, saying, "I need one too to settle my nerves after what I've just been through." He then proceeded to tell them the story of the night's event from the Masons' perspective. As I listened I had visions of middle-aged men, dressed in strange garb, jumping about in a manner similar to the jumping of the exploding firecrackers. I was amazed at the ability of Mum and her friends to maintain straight faces during Dad's tale, and to offer such seemingly innocent comments as, "Oh, don't tell me that!" or "Oh, no. I can't believe it." I imagine they would have exchanged a few kicks and nudges under the table as well.

Later that week the story appeared in the local paper, and when Dad passed the paper to Mum to read the article, she blanched and looked much in need of another brandy. Dad never did learn of Mum's part in this escapade, but his time in the Masons was short-lived, as he soon found that their rituals were not his cup of tea.

Another frequent source of entertainment in my youth was the local dance, held almost every Saturday night, at one or other of the district halls (Biloela, Thangool, Lorgie etc.), with a much less frequent but more pretentious "Ball" held to mark some particular event in the local calendar, such as the Annual Biloela and District Show. In another chapter I shall describe the usual format of these dances, and how one in particular remains lodged in my memory.

Another particular dance that sticks in my mind is one in which it was decided, by those who organised these weekly events, that it might be fun if, for a change, the boys dressed up as and acted the part of girls, while the girls adopted the dress and manner of boys. I understand that the motivation behind this move was the fact that many of the women who regularly attended these dances had a deep-seated fear of becoming wallflowers. They were also becoming tired of the feeling of embarrassment they experienced when, having waited patiently for the young men to arrive after the pubs closed at 10:00 pm, they would find themselves the objects of close, critical scrutiny, often followed by rejection, by half-drunk youths, whenever the MC called "Gentlemen, select your partners" for whatever dance was next on the programme. It apparently did not occur to these women, at that point, that some of the males experienced an equal measure of embarrassment when their requests for the pleasure of a dance were rejected by a female with her hopes pinned on a more attractive potential partner.

In any event, the novel idea of gender swapping for the purposes of a dance was readily embraced by the dancing populace, and the date was set, with prizes offered for the best turned out male/female, and female/male participants.

On the day of the dance, my mother and I found ourselves run off our feet in Mum's hairdressing salon by young bucks seeking to have their hair curled and set for the event, with their eyes set on the prize offered. With their generally short haircuts, we employed pin curlers and butterfly clips, with generous applications of setting gel, to create curls and waves. This necessitated the customers' departure for several hours with their curlers and clips in place, to allow the setting gel to do its work, before returning later in the day to have the implements removed and their hair brushed up into a style.

One of these young men worked at a local service station. In those days there was no such thing as self service, and the service station attendant would fill the customer's car with petrol, clean the windscreen, and check the oil, water, tyres and battery, while the customer relaxed in the vehicle. When this lad returned to our salon late in the afternoon to have his hairdo completed, he told us with considerable amusement how a passing traveller had stared at him, mouth agape, when he came out to service his car with his hair in curlers. "Wait till he goes around town and sees all the other blokes with curlers in their hair," he added. "He'll wonder what's going on in this weird joint!" he concluded.

When the dance got under way that evening, there was much merriment as we witnessed many of the boys tottering along unsteadily on high heels, some struggling with long frocks, and others displaying hairy legs beneath their shorter skirts. It appeared that they had drawn the line at shaving their legs. Many of the girls also looked hilarious in their men's suits, borrowed from father, brother or male friend, with belts tightened up around their chests, trousers overlapping at the front, and jackets hanging down, in some cases almost to their ankles, with sleeves pinned up at the wrist. There was also, apparently, a good deal of chiacking in the pub when some of the braver lads breasted up to the bar in their frocks to demand a beer. One barmaid is reported to have loudly proclaimed, "No women served in the bar, ladies. The lounge at the back is at your disposal."

As my mind wanders back over these events, and I picture the young people frolicking about on the dance floor, I feel myself beginning to drift into sleep, so I put down my pen, turn off my bedside light, and settle down for the night, with the sweet familiar refrain of "The Tennessee Waltz" wafting through my head.

The Wheels of Progress

Just before retiring tonight I emptied our dishwasher, which set me thinking about how different life now is to how it was in the early post-war years, when we did not have available to us the multitude of labour-saving devices that modern technology provides. Despite those technological advantages, we do not seem to have more time now for active recreation and family life than we had in those former times. Perhaps that is because, in order to acquire all those "advantages", we have to work longer hours, or perhaps it is merely that we have become addicted to the soft, easy option of spending many of our leisure hours watching the television shows to which we have become addicted.

I can still remember when mains-power electricity first came to Biloela. That event generated enormous excitement amongst the small local population. The girl who had been chosen as "Queen" of Biloela at the recent debutantes' ball was carried through the streets on the back of a table-top truck, decorated with balloons and streamers. She was attended by suitably dressed handmaidens. All this was preceded by a small brass band with marching girls. The entire population turned out to cheer, wave banners and throw streamers. There was dancing and singing in the streets until dawn.

The arrival of electricity to the town was not matched by the introduction of sewerage. The old earth closet outback "dunnies" continued to dot the landscape for many years afterwards. These were invariably situated as far from the back door of each residence as the size of the allotment would allow, to ensure that the unpleasant odour that surrounded them remained remote from the living quarters. Even places of public resort, like the dance halls, were serviced by such outdoor facilities.

As I think now about those inconvenient conveniences, I cannot imagine how we females managed to negotiate them when dressed up in our finery, with full skirts and multiple starched petticoats, which were the height of fashion in those days. As every dance got into full swing there would invariably develop a line-up of women waiting to use the toilets, all chatting excitedly about the goings-on in the hall, or which boys they found most attractive, or just generally about clothes or life's recent events. Occasionally, if one became desperate to do a number one, and she was still well away from the head of the queue, she would dart off to the side into a darker area where she would squat down behind a bush to relieve herself, while a couple of her friends stood guard to warn of the approach of any stray males. This was a scary process, as there was the ever present fear of snakes or other crawly things, and even if touched on the bare bottom by an unseen blade of grass, there would be a shriek and a leap from the urinator which would be immediately imitated by her guardian friends. The whole group would then scarper off together giggling uncontrollably.

At our home, in those days, we always seemed to have friends, either my sister's or mine, and often my parents', staying with us. The single outback toilet was still required to service us all. Whenever a call of nature arose at night for one of the female members of the house, she would take a torch and, accompanied by at least one, and often more, of the other female residents, she would make the trek to the "dunny". This was the opportunity for a little private female chatter and, in Mum's case, also for a secret cigarette, as Dad frowned very much upon women smoking. She would take a small bottle of perfume with her, with which she would dab herself liberally after her cigarette to camouflage the smell. Sometimes she even went as far as to place a drop on her tongue, to sweeten her breath.

These nightly excursions were sometimes undertaken by the married female participants as a pretext for the sole purpose of exchanging grumbles about their husbands. It was also not unknown for one of us to sneak out after them to hide behind the toilet, or elsewhere in the backyard, to jump out and scream in order to scare the living daylights out of the one emerging from the toilet.

One of my early jobs was as a waitress at one of Biloela's two hotels. There we enjoyed the luxury of indoor toilets connected to a septic tank. Little did I realise when I started there and began to experience that relative luxury that it would be later curtailed by an extraordinary event that no-one could foresee, and which I shall subsequently relate.

My job at the hotel was a very busy one as, in addition to waiting at table in the dining room, my fellow waitress (a close friend) and I were required to set the tables, wash and dry the dishes, clean the kitchen and dining room, launder the tea-towels, shine up the silverware so that it sparkled on the dining tables and generally help out around the place as required. Before mealtime we would dress up in our starched white uniforms which we would have laundered and ironed ourselves, the ironing being accomplished with what was then a modern, high-tech implement in the form of a petrol heated iron.

Despite the work-load, I enjoyed the job, particularly the interaction with the patrons that was part of waitressing. The hotel had a number of permanent guests, including, at one time, a local dentist, some bank officers and a crop-duster pilot, as well as a regular turnover of casual guests, mostly travelling salesmen or other business people. We got to know the permanents fairly well, and sometimes, after dinner, they would join us on the verandah outside for a chat and a few laughs. Sometimes I even managed to con one of them into helping us with the washing-up and drying of the dishes, particularly if my friend and I were in a hurry to get away to attend a dance or the local picture show.

I recall one occasion when I was serving a business man and his colleagues, and we had both lamb and mutton on the menu. Being a bit of a smartie, he asked me what was the difference between the lamb and the mutton. In my innocence, and knowing that they were both in fact cut from the same joint of meat (undoubtedly mutton!), I gave him a puzzled look and, pointing at the menu, said, "See. The lamb comes with mint sauce, and the mutton with gravy."

I did not then understand why that response evoked so much laughter from the men at his table, and when I reported the incident to the cook she scolded me for my ignorance.

After a time the hotel changed hands, and the new female proprietor, who ran the house, attempted to introduce rankings among the staff (first waitress, second waitress, etc.). It appeared to us that she was trying to divide and conquer us, but that was not very successful as we were all too close. My fellow waitress and I, being fairly typical young teenagers, were constantly giggling at the slightest thing, which was a source of constant annoyance to her.

One good thing the new boss did was to hire an extra girl to help with the more menial tasks. This girl came from a very large farming family, and was quite shy and naive. She was like a fish out of water in the hotel environment. My fellow waitress and I tended to show off our own perceived sophistication in front of her.

One day, having been given the task of washing the dirty tea-towels in the external copper boiler, our country recruit came to us in tears, with a cup in her hand. She told us the boss had verbally abused her for using a good cup to measure out the soap powder, and instructed her to obtain a cracked or chipped one from the kitchen for that purpose. There being no cracked or chipped cups immediately to be seen in the kitchen, I took the cup she was holding from her hand and rapped it quickly against the edge of the sink to crack it, and handed it back to her with a smile, saying, "If she wants a cracked cup, here's one now!" She stared at me in disbelief, with a horrified look on her face. My friend and I then began to giggle, and my friend immediately grabbed another good cup which she proceeded to crack in the same manner as I had. I then repeated the dose with a third. Between us we thus cracked or chipped four or five cups, which we placed on a shelf in the kitchen "for future use", all whilst giggling continuously. From that moment we were our country cousin's heroines, and she became our constant shadow.

Another interesting member of the hotel staff was a yardman (whom I shall call "Billy"). He had some permanent brain damage, which we were told was from alcohol, but I really do not know the truth or falsity of that. He was a good worker, but his speech was very hard to understand until you became accustomed to it. He had a rather childish sense of humour, and often pretended to chase we girls about, or otherwise join in our silliness.

One day, for reasons which remain totally unknown to me, he apparently threw an explosive device of some kind into the hotel's septic tank, causing a loud explosion, followed by a shower of debris, including shit, which peppered the hotel, the adjoining laneway and adjacent buildings, creating a harsh jangle of noise as it rained down on their tin roofs. Later, rumour circulated that one of the town's snobbiest ladies had been walking along the laneway at the crucial moment, wearing one of the expensive, large picture hats that she was known to favour, and became covered in shit from head to toe.

The resultant stench in the immediate vicinity lasted for several weeks, and made working in the hotel almost unbearable. The boss did provide us with some crude cloth face masks, which she cut out from old sheets, and which she doused with perfume to alleviate the smell, but these were only minimally effective. For many months after that event it was a standing joke amongst the local population to ask each other where they were "when the shit hit the fan".

After that smell had faded somewhat, it was a little reminiscent of the smell of animal droppings that usually accompanied a visit by a travelling circus. That was a big event in the life of a small country town like Biloela. On a shopping excursion today I passed a circus, set up in a park in a nearby suburb. I hardly gave it a second glance, although I did notice there was no sign of the caged animals and tethered elephants that were such a feature of those earlier circus visits. In addition, this circus looked relatively lifeless, with very few people about. That, too, contrasted sharply with the excitement and hubbub that surrounded the circus visits of my youth.

I remember how they would enter the town in a cavalcade of trucks and trailers, with an attended elephant often leading the way. Brightly dressed trapeze artists would be strutting and pirouetting to the beat of a drum, or the sound of a brass band, and tumblers and clowns would parade their talents to the multitude of townsfolk who had turned out to watch this spectacle. Shopkeepers and shoppers would pour out of the shops onto the streets to join the crowds already gathering to witness this rare and lively event.

We young girls would rush home as soon as we could to put on our prettiest dresses, with their full skirts and wide belts, do our hair and makeup, and then rush down in a group to watch the erection of the circus tent. In reality, we were there not so much to watch the miracle of the Big-Top rising as to ogle the bulging muscles of the often bare-chested young men who swung their sledgehammers so easily to drive in the large stakes needed to hold the tent stays. We would shamelessly flirt with this new male blood in town, as they would flirt with us in return, and deliberately flex their muscles for our admiration. Then we would walk around to inspect the poor caged animals, usually a few lions and a handful of monkeys, and gaze at the grazing ponies and the lumbering elephants. The latter were either being used as beasts of burden in the preparation work, or stood, tethered by one leg, and swaying back and forth to their own inner rhythm.

That night, the whole town would turn out to see the show. There would be a long line-up for admission tickets, and as we entered the tent we would load ourselves up with confectionery, like popcorn, peanuts, toffee-apples or fairy-floss, and rush to grab the hard, bench-type seats nearest to the sawdust covered circus ring. There we would sit, careless of the physical discomfort, enjoying the build-up of excitement that preceded the eventual appearance of the ring-master, with the booming voice and grand manner, who would introduce each act using grandiose terms such as "never previously attempted", or "the only one of its kind in the world" or "death-defying". We would then watch, wide-eyed, as each performance unfolded: through the choreographed movements of the roaring lions controlled by a single lion-tamer armed with only a whip and a chair; the prancing, decorated ponies ridden by clever, agile monkeys; the amazing elephants who could lift enormous weights yet balance delicately on a large wooden ball or a small, upside down, timber tub; the comical antics of juggling and tumbling clowns; all culminating in a thrilling trapeze act through which we would hold our breaths in fearful anticipation of a fall by one of those daring, skilful artists.

After the show concluded, we would wend our way home, full of excited chatter about the wonder of it all, and debating the relative merits of the various acts we had witnessed. That would be the primary topic of conversation amongst the populace for several days afterwards.

Travelling circuses of that kind are a rarity these days, having been overshadowed and eventually displaced by large, free-range animal parks and zoos, and the ready availability to all of the spectacular , world-class show productions which are so regularly featured either on television or at the cinema.

The cinema, too, has changed dramatically since my youthful days in Biloela. At that time there were no wide screens or stereophonic, surround-sound systems so standard in modern cinemas, and "digital" was simply a word that signified something to do with fingers or toes, and had nothing to do with technology. Whilst we, the audience, sat in our canvas seats, the projectionist sat up behind in a small projection room, hand feeding reels of film into a projector with a powerful light source to project the moving images onto the comparatively small, square, flat screen at the front of the theatre. The sound tracks of these films were sometimes marred by loud crackling noises making it difficult to fully comprehend the dialogue.

Not infrequently there would be a breakdown in the projection, usually brought about by a break in the celluloid film, and there would be a pause of uncertain length while the projectionist struggled to repair it and re-thread the film through the projector. During these pauses, the young blades in the audience would vie with each other to see who could come up with the smartest wise-crack to shout at the top of his voice, and someone would nearly always shine a torchlight onto the screen to project finger images for his and others' amusement. Sometimes, even when the film was running, some clown would shine a torch at the screen, which would provoke the theatre proprietor to hurry down the aisle with his own torch in search of the culprit who, if found, would be summarily ejected. But by that time the culprit would generally have turned off their torch and hidden it under their shirt or skirt, to the frustration of the proprietor and the general amusement of the younger members of the audience.

The layout and construction of the theatre also lent itself to a bit of fun and games unrelated to the film on show. For example, the paired, canvas seats were ideal for lovers more interested in necking than watching the movie. I fondly recall some of my own indulgences in that youthful pastime. The timber floor which sloped slightly towards the front provided a race for the younger members of the audience to roll their empty soft-drink bottles down, if bored, at crucial or tense moments of the film. Towards the rear of the theatre was a raised balcony, with padded leather seats instead of the canvas ones, tickets to which were more expensive, and which were favoured by both older patrons and younger ones who were more class-conscious. This apparent class divide occasionally led to some generally good-natured banter between members of the different groups.

At this point, my unusually lengthy reminiscences are interrupted by the ringing of my telephone. As I know it will be my husband, Travis, ringing from Sydney, before going to bed, I put down my pen, and hurry to enjoy a few words with him before finally going to sleep, with visions of old movies intermingling with my early dreams.

A Dash of Show-Business

Once again, tonight, as I settle down for my nocturnal writing ritual, it is something I saw and did today that takes me back to my youth. But that is not through any perceived similarity between the two eras, but rather because of the contrast.

I spent some time shopping at our local Shopping Town Mall, where I was struck by the fact that there seemed to be dozens of clothing boutiques, all side by side, each displaying rack upon rack of modern, trendy women's-wear. I soon found myself in one of those boutiques flipping through dozens of frocks, of many different styles and colours. It was not that I was really looking for something special, or specific, but one caught my eye, and I tried it on. I liked it, but there were two quite distinct colours available, and I couldn't choose between them. So, I pulled out my credit card, and bought both. Somehow, it still does not quite feel like spending money when I debit an amount to my credit card. I have great difficulty explaining that to my husband when the statement comes at the end of the month.

In my teenage and early adult years, in Biloela, there were only one or two women's-wear shops in town, and they had a very limited supply of ready-made frocks. If we were lucky enough to find one that we liked, and that fitted us, we would generally pay a small deposit in cash, and the storekeeper would put the article aside in what was called "lay-by". We would then pay it off by small instalments over several weeks before we were able to take it home. There were no such things as credit cards, and only the wealthiest of citizens were able to run credit accounts at the town's stores. More often, we would buy material from a drapery and have the frock made up from a pattern either by our mothers or a dress-maker. Some girls (of which I was not one!) even made their own .

When some social event, like the annual district show (which was probably the biggest social event of the year) was in prospect, we would hunt through women's magazines for styles that appealed to us, both for a day dress to wear to the show and an evening gown for the Ball. Then we would search the drapery shops for suitable patterns and materials to provide to the dress-maker. I believe it was this preparation, and the ultimate dressing-up that generated the most excitement for we young females, rather than the events themselves.

On show day we would dress in our new finery, come rain, hail or shine, and excitedly pick our way through dust or mud, depending on the weather, often having to dodge cow-pats, to watch such events as the buck-jumping, or the wood chopping, or to inspect the various displays in the pavilion, or to embark upon some of the fun rides available. There were also a few tawdry sideshows to attract us. If a girl had a beau, he would usually accompany her and try to win for her some of the prizes, like soft toys or sweets that were on offer in the game stalls which lined the sideshow alleyways. If a girl did not have a beau, there were always young bucks about who were keen to try to impress the unattached females with their skill and prowess at the games in those stalls, and to offer them any prizes won, in the hope of winning a date.

I recall one particular show at which my Dad became involved in the boxing/wrestling side-show, which was operated by a long-term acquaintance of his. In advance of the show, Dad and a wild Irish friend cooked up a scheme to attract customers to the boxing tent. This scheme involved their staging a very public, verbal brawl in the town, with a couple of stooges to hold them apart while they mouthed obscenities and threats at each other. This charade culminated in one of them loudly challenging the other to a no-holds-barred wrestling match in the boxing tent at the show, with some invented prize at stake.

Before the show day arrived, Dad and his Irish friend made detailed plans, in our kitchen, about how their bout would unfold. They practised various wrestling holds on each other, and ways to appear to break those holds. Dad's friend had a beard at that time, and one of the tricks they dreamt up was for him to hide some bindy-eye prickles in his beard, which Dad would grab early in the bout, only to yell in pain, and then become enraged when his fingers contacted those prickles.

When the big day arrived, we all fronted up outside the boxing tent at the appointed time. One of Dad's jobs was to stand on the raised platform in front of the tent banging on a big base drum to "drum up" crowd interest, while his friend, the side-show operator, spruiked to the gathering audience about the prowess of the members of his troupe, and what was going to happen in the tent once the audience had paid up their admission fee and gained entry to it. He had a number of semi-professional boxers and wrestlers in his entourage, and called for challengers from the crowd to take on each of them, in turn, over 2 or 3 rounds of boxing or wrestling. There was no shortage of willing takers for that challenge amongst the local lads anxious to show off their own real or imagined fighting qualities. He also gave a verbal build-up for the "grudge match" to occur between Dad and his Irish mate, with each of them exchanging loud verbal barbs about what they would do to each other once the bout began.

In due course, the protagonists entered the tent, followed by a large crowd of excited, paying customers. When their turn on the programme came (as the last bout of the day), Dad and his mate put on a good show, much to the enjoyment of the enthusiastic spectators. At the end of three gruelling rounds, both were looking exhausted, but neither showed signs of surrendering. The operator declared it a draw, and called upon the two contestants to shake hands, saying, "You've been mates for too many years not to put this row behind you now." Although they at first feigned reluctance to do so, they eventually did as he asked. That brought a roar of approval from the crowd. The two then left the ring with their arms around each other's shoulders, once again the best of mates, and waving to the cheering audience.

Writing about show-business reminds me of another vicarious association with shows that I subsequently experienced.

Some years after the show events to which I have already referred, when I was working for a time in my mother's hairdressing salon in Biloela, I got to know a very well-dressed, nicely-spoken lady, of about my mother's age, who ran a recently opened "Dairy Queen" shop a few doors down the street from our salon. She was the wife of a very tall, distinguished looking man who had come to Biloela to manage the newly formed Callide-Dawson Co-0perative Bacon Society. I gradually got to know this lady through my regular visits to her shop for ice-cream, or sandwiches and coffee for our lunches. At that time, little did I realize that I would eventually work for her, and that, even later, she and her husband would become my parents-in-law.

As I came to know her better, and regaled her with stories of my father's show exploits (not just in Biloela, but also earlier at many shows, including the Brisbane Exhibition) as a vendor of toffee-apples and fairy-floss, she eventually disclosed to me that she, too, had something of a show-business background. She told me how her mother, father, one brother and herself had spent part of the depression years travelling as "showies" to various shows throughout New South Wales, Victoria and South Australia, presenting a show built around magic performed by her brother, with her acting as his assistant. As well as the usual conjuring tricks involving card reading, disappearing and reappearing birds, balls and the like, there were two particular tricks in which she participated quite actively, which were very popular with the audiences.

In one, she would enter a large cage on the stage and, after a few waves of her brother's "magic" cloak, she would suddenly disappear from the audience's view, leaving the cage apparently empty. Then, when her brother enunciated some "magic words", and waved his cloak again in front of the cage, she would mysteriously reappear.

In another, she would kneel and position her neck on what appeared to be the base of a guillotine, with its shiny blade suspended above. Her brother would then cover her head with a cloth, but so that the audience could still see her kneeling body on the other side of the guillotine. After some "magical" passes of his cloak and a few incantations, he would quickly bring down the blade of the guillotine to apparently sever her head from her body. As the audience gasped in horror, they would see the cloth covering her head drop into a basket below the guillotine with a loud thud, simulating the sound of her falling, severed head. But, after a moment of stunned silence from the audience, her brother would again wave his cloak, and she would stand up behind the guillotine, her head still firmly attached to her shoulders. From the basket she would then retrieve a large head of cabbage. She never fully explained to me how the trick was done, except to say that it was "all smoke and mirrors", and that the blade of the guillotine was hinged so that it retracted into the frame when lowered.

She also told me that she had been a singer and a dancer in her youth particularly in Highland dancing (at which her mother had excelled), but also in ballet and tap. During the war, she had taken part, both as performer in and the production of some local concerts to raise funds for The Australian Comforts Fund, an organisation that put together and sent comfort packages to our armed servicemen overseas, which included her own husband on active service in New Guinea. She also did something similar, but for the local chamber of commerce, after the war, in another country town where her husband conducted a butchery business. She proudly told me that her son, my future husband, had participated as a performer in that concert.

Later, she became involved as dancing instructor in a musical concert held in Biloela. She taught some of the local girls to perform a ballet routine that she choreographed. A local man acted as MC, and also performed comical acts to fill in between the various musical presentations. He dressed in a rather tattered, comical outfit, with a hole in the back of his trousers. All went well until, nearing the end of the concert, he had the notion to turn his trousers back-to-front in order to enhance his comic appearance. The back-stage lighting being rather dim, he failed to notice that, with his trousers reversed, his penis became visible from the front upon certain movements. In the much brighter light on the stage, when he appeared and was jigging about telling his jokes, his private parts were displayed to the audience. Many of them found that quite amusing, and laughed raucously, which he mistook for appreciation of his jokes, and was encouraged to continue. Seeing what was really happening, my future father-in-law, and some others, frantically signalled to him to leave the stage, but this too he mistook for encouragement, and continued his antics. Eventually, he appeared to get the message, and left the stage, where he was informed of his faux pas. No doubt that was one of the most embarrassing moments of his life, but he tried valiantly to put it behind him and carefully re-adjusted his trousers for the grand finale.

The townsfolk dined out on that piece of misadventure for several days afterwards, but the gentleman in question brazened it out, and the incident eventually faded into history, just as I am ready, now, to fade into sleep.

First Romance

As I prepare for bed tonight, I think how late it is again. I had an old friend from Biloela visit me today, and we sat up late, over a glass of wine, talking over each other as we each tried to get in first with what we wanted to say. I have enjoyed her company, and will miss her when she goes.

One of the things we talked about was how, in the country, we always had animals of one kind or another around, as house pets. Apart from dogs, about which I shall say more shortly, it was not unusual for Dad to bring home some more exotic animal from one of his frequent country trips.

At one time, when Mum was running her hairdressing salon from the verandah of our small home, Dad brought home a kangaroo. Although it was a beautiful creature, and quite playful at times, it also had a rather pugnacious disposition, particularly towards strangers. Quite a few visitors to Mum's salon were accosted by this feisty bounder, and challenged to a fight. That was not a challenge to which anyone was disposed to respond, and some retreated in fear. Eventually, Dad was prevailed upon to return the pugilistic roo to the farm from which he came.

Another of the more exotic pets Dad brought home was an emu. It, too, proved a handful to manage around the house and salon, to which it did not really encourage the return of customers. So, once again, Dad had to take it back to the farm.

A more successful pet acquisition was a beautiful Rosella. Mum taught it to do a very impressive wolf-whistle, which it would produce whenever a female approached. Many of Mum's salon customers enjoyed that approving sound as they emerged with their new hair styles, as did others just walking by our house. Strangely, that bird never did whistle at a male person.

Later, after Mum had moved her hairdressing salon to a shop in the main street, we acquired, first, my little Foxie dog, Soda, and later, a Great Dane, whose name I cannot now recall, but which I shall call Brutus.

Before the arrival of Brutus, Soda (who habitually followed me everywhere around town) had been intimidated by a rather noisy, aggressive, much larger dog that lived at the house on the corner not far from our house. After the arrival of Brutus, it, too, adopted the habit of accompanying me (and Soda) on our journeys around town. Although Brutus was a very placid, friendly dog, its sheer size intimidated many, including other dogs. Little Soda quickly adapted to the presence of this gigantic addition to our household, and the two soon became firm friends. Soda also quickly perceived that Brutus had other dogs, including his former nemesis on the corner, bluffed. Now, as we walked past this corner residence, Soda would noisily challenge its resident mastiff with a volley of loud barks and, when this beast poked its nose out in response, Soda would take refuge under the belly, and between the legs of Brutus, from where he would continue his challenge to the other dog, which could only growl in frustration whilst keeping a safe distance from its tormentor and his giant protector.

Another slightly less endearing habit of Soda's was to try to follow me to the local dances. Although I was mostly successful in dissuading him, there were a couple of occasions when, despite my best efforts, he turned up at the dancehall . Fortunately, Brutus exhibited no inclination to follow Soda's lead in this respect. Once there, Soda would not leave my side, and whenever I attempted to dance, he would take a corner of the hem of my frock in his teeth and tug at it, playfully, as I tried to whirl or glide, as appropriate, in the course of the dance. Besides being highly embarrassing to me, I went home with holes in the bottom of my skirt from Soda's teeth.

As I am writing this, I have become aware of a scratching noise which, after a moment, I realise is made by a branch rubbing against the window outside my bedroom. If I were alone tonight that noise would scare me silly, so I find it comforting that I have someone else in the house.

However, as I lie there listening to this scratching noise I am reminded of another earlier time when I was sitting on my bed in the little fibro house and I heard a similar scratching noise, which was coming from under my bed. As I looked under the bed I saw it was my little dog, Soda, making the noise, with short sharp convulsive movements. I realized instantly that there was something terribly wrong with him, and as I gently pulled him out from under my bed his little face looked up at me sadly, and his eyes seemed to say: "Can't you do something to help me?"

In panic I ran to the garage next door to call the boy I knew who worked there. He came running to my aid, in the company of a young farmer I had seen around town, but didn't know, who happened to be having some work done at the garage at that moment.

"What's the matter? What's the matter with Soda" I cried.

They exchanged knowing looks, and one said: "It looks like some mongrel has poisoned him. We'd better get him off to the vet as quick as we can. You stay here, we'll take him for you, and let you know what happens as soon as we can."

It seemed ages, but was really only a few minutes before they returned with the sad news that my Soda was dead. I cried for days, and thought I would never get over it. Then one day the young farmer turned up on my doorstep with a young pup, one of the litter his bitch had just given birth to on the farm. As I hugged my new-found pet (which I later christened "Whisky") I gave the kind young farmer a second look. "Not bad!" I said to myself. I was then overcome by shyness as I felt my first flutter of attraction to a boy. I was to see more of him later.

By this time Dad had started in Real-Estate, and was doing quite well selling local farming properties. He and Mum decided to build their first home, about which they were very excited.

I remember when we were packing up to move to our new home. I found Soda's old food bowl, with his name "Soda" scratched into the side with a nail. My feeling of sadness returned briefly, and it was then that I decided to call my new pup "Whisky", to go with "Soda", and quickly scratched his name into the bowl too.

As we left the old fibro house I recall looking back, and as I saw the low, dilapidated wire mesh fence, with grass growing through it, I started to laugh. Dad said: "What are you laughing at?" I said: "Nothing". "That girl's mad, she laughs at nothing" said Dad.

What I was thinking about, but didn't tell him, was the time when my friend Janet and I were on our way home one night from the local dance. As we got to the corner of the garage, next to our house, a girl (Betty) who lived a couple of doors down from us, was just standing there.

"What are you standing here for" I asked.

"Shh" she said "I just saw a prowler in a long overcoat go into your yard."

As I followed her back to our front yard, I saw a tall man, in a long coat, standing in the middle of the pathway leading to the house, staring in our direction.

"I'm off" said Betty, and did a bolt towards her house.

Janet and I stood there, too scared to go forward, but not knowing what else to do.

"Let's wait here until someone comes along" I said. "The Baker boys should be coming this way soon. They were at the dance. We'll grab hold of the first man who comes this way and ask him to take us in."

Just then we saw one of the Baker boys coming along the street. We raced up to him, and I said:

"Will you take us to our front door? There's a prowler in our yard. There he is over there" I said, pointing in the prowler's direction.

At that very moment, we saw the prowler jump over the low fence from our yard into the street, heading in our direction. The Baker boy took off in the opposite direction, and as I grabbed his arm I yelled to Janet: "Hang onto him Janet, as long as we have hold of something that looks like a man, we should be O.K.".

"Tell it to the bloody marines" replied Janet, at the same time grabbing our bodyguard's other arm.

We found it hard to keep up with our saviour, who was in full stride by now, but we each held onto an arm with all our might, as we trailed along behind yelling and screaming.

The Baker boy managed to pull his arms out of his coat, leaving Janet and I grasping his empty jacket as we tumbled and fell on top of each other to the ground, still screaming as he disappeared into the night.

Just then, I heard a voice calling "Cynthia, Cynthia, are you all right?"

I recognized the voice as that of my brother-in-law, and then it dawned on me that he was our "prowler".

"What were you doing standing there in our yard. You looked like a prowler" I said angrily.

"I was trying to save your neck" he said, "because if your Dad wakes up and finds you not home yet you'll be in hot water. I was looking out for you. Anyway, what was going on there? I thought you were being attacked by some bloke, that's why I jumped the fence."

"No" I replied. "It was just one of the Baker boys. We were trying to hang onto him for protection from you."

At that point, Janet and I began to see the funny side and broke into uncontrollable giggles, which frustrated my brother-in-law no end. He kept telling us to "shut up" or we would be in "big strife" if we woke up Dad, as we should have been in hours ago.

Try as we might, we could not stop our giggling, and buried our faces in our pillows as soon as we got inside, with my brother-in-law continually saying "Shh, shh, you'll wake Tom". Fortunately, he slept through it, and never heard the story.

After we moved into our new house, one night, when Mum worked late in her shop, she asked me and a friend of mine to close up the shop for her, while she raced home to get tea ready. Just as we closed the door, two boys cruising by in their FJ Holden stopped. One was the young farmer who had helped me out with "Soda" and brought me "Whisky".

"Would you like a lift home?" the driver asked.

"Yeah" we replied.

My friend jumped into the front seat, with the driver, and I sat behind with the farmer boy who had made my heart flutter a few months before. On the way to my friends place, the young farmer said to me:

"I'm comin into town again next Wen'sdy, would ya like to go to the pitchers Wen'sdy night?"

"O.K." I said, without worrying about what Dad would say. "I'll worry about that later", I thought to myself.

No sooner had we pulled up outside my friend's place than a car screeched to a halt beside us. My God, it was Dad, and he was mad. It was 7.30 at night and here I was sitting in a car beside a boy!

"Get into this car, girl" he yelled to me. I did as I was told. We then drove home in stoney silence. I thought to myself: "I don't have to worry about asking his permission to go out on Wednesday night, that'll be the end of that romance."

Much to my surprise, the boy turned up on our doorstep on the following Wednesday night. Dad took him outside for a talk. I said to Mum:

"God, What's he saying to him?" Mum said: "I told him to apologize, because he is a very nice boy and you are lucky to have him interested in you."

Why is it that our mothers always thought we were lucky to attract a man, and our father's acted as if we had committed a criminal act?

After that shaky start, that boy became my steady boy-friend for a time.

One day when I was working in Mum's shop, a couple of girls who worked across the road came running in, breathless with excitement.

"Get a load of the 2 good sorts who have just hit town", one said, as we all rushed to the window to look out.

Two new lads were walking down the street, one tall and dark, the other shorter and fair. They looked as if they were aware of all the eyes on them, and were enjoying it.

"Get a load of the tall one" said one "I bags him".

"He looks like he thinks he's God's gift to women. I like the shorter one", I said. At that moment I had a premonition that that was the boy I was going to marry.

When I told Mum about my premonition, she said:

"Don't be stupid. You've got a nice boy. You couldn't get a nicer one. You should put your best foot forward, or you might lose him, if you go talking like that."

I said: "I don't care".

She said: "I don't know what's thc matter with that girl".

Later that night, thinking about the boy I had seen through my window on the world, I asked Mum and Dad how they met.

"My sister Doreen had a pretty good looking friend she kept telling me about" said Dad, "who turned out to be your mother. She introduced us at a local dance, and I thought 'Wow!', and tried to get every dance with her. As usual, the local lads were popping in and out of the dance to sample their grog supplies which they kept in a car boot outside. Meanwhile, a group of Main Roads workers who were camped nearby were taking the opportunity to get in under their necks with the local girls. Needless to say it all ended up in a blue. Doreen yelled to your mother to hang onto me, because she knew I liked a good stoush and was always one of the first to have a go. She hung onto me so tight, I couldn't get loose to join the fight."

"You didn't bloody struggle too hard" Mum interrupted. "You didn't mind me hanging onto you".

"Well, I didn't have many opportunities in them days to have a good lookin sheila hang onto me so tight. I was usually doin' the hanging on. You knew a good thing to hang onto when you got the chance" he said.

"Don't kid y'self" said Mum, "I was just doin' ya a favour. You'd a had ya head punched in".

"They'd have to be pretty bloody good to punch my head in" said Dad.

At that point I left the room. I was sorry I'd asked. They were still going 5 minutes later. I thought this could end up in one of their rows, so I cleared out to my sister's place next door.

Dad's description of the dance at which he met Mum reminded me of the dances we attended, which were not much different. The girls would arrive at the scheduled starting time, dressed in their best clothes, and sit around on the long stools in their full skirts with layer upon layer of starched petti-coats, waiting for the boys to arrive. A few boys would gradually straggle in, and congregate near the door, dashing in and out, to either visit the pub across the street, or (in the case of a bush dance) to hang around the open car boot parked outside. A few brave boys would even front the dance floor with the girls, but mostly the girls who wanted to dance at that stage of the evening had to dance with each other.

The dance would only really get started after 10pm when the pub shut, or the car-boot was emptied, and the boys would descend on the dance hall in numbers, full of dutch courage from the grog, yahoohing and showing off for the benefit of the girls. The dancing would then become more vigorous, as the night progressed, with each couple trying to outdo the others by making the most noise, and having the biggest slide to thump into the wall at one end of the hall, and then the other, in their favourite dance, "The Gipsy Tap".

When the "supper dance" was announced, there would be a mad rush by the boys to select the most popular girls, in order to have the opportunity to take them in to supper, which was like a reservation to escort them home after the dance. Then when the music stopped, there would be another rush to be the first couple into the supper room, which was a point of honour with the boys for some reason. Occasionally, a boy who was jealous of another's choice of supper partner would project a dollop of cream, or a morsel of cake, in his rival's direction, using his fork or spoon as a sling-shot. This sometimes led to a generalised food fight, in which all and sundry joined with gusto. To see all those beautiful cakes and biscuits, so lovingly prepared and donated by the local CWA women, tossed about, was a shame, but everyone seemed to have a good time.

Most nights there was at least one fist fight, which would erupt either just inside or outside the door of the hall, between rival boys who had had too much to drink, or had too much youthful energy. Someone would shout: "There's a beaut fight on out there", and we would all rush out to see what was going on. There were usually more punches thrown than landed, and after a little blood was spilt, someone would step in and break it up, saying to the combatants: "Shake hands now, its all over", and they would. We would all then troop back inside to continue the dance.

It was at one of these dances that I first came face to face with the boy I had seen through Mum's shop window some time earlier walking down the street with his taller brother. His parents had apparently not long before moved into town. I had forgotten my premonition at that stage, when he asked me to dance. He told me he was on holidays from the University, in Brisbane. Although it felt good dancing with him, I was suspicious of him because he came from the city. After a bit of small talk, he put his cheek against mine. I thought: "This clown must have babies all over Brisbane", so I immediately asked him to sit me down, which he did, looking puzzled. At the time I didn't realize how much my life was going to change as a result of my meeting with that boy.

With that thought, I look across at the clock. It's late. I have to have an early start tomorrow, to get my friend off on her way home. I reach for the light switch, already thinking about tomorrow.

Clipped Wings

To-night, as I prepare for bed, I feel strongly the absence of my friend, after having her company last night. Once more I am aware of the night noises, which seemed to go into hiding while she was here. It's as if the night creatures know I am alone again, and have come out to play on my nerves. Again I seek refuge in penning my thoughts.

My mind goes back to this morning. After the hustle and bustle of my friend's early departure, I decided to go for a walk along the track by the creek. It was such a lovely crisp morning. As I felt the coolness of the air on my face, and drew the lapels of my jacket together across my chest I thought how much I love the early morning. It reminds me of the time when I was a boarder at the Sisters of Mercy Convent, in the small country town, Biloela. One of the jobs which the Sisters gave me was to escort one of the younger boarders down to the post office in the town where she would be picked up by the cream carrier to go home to her parent's farm for boarders' weekends. We would have to leave the convent at about 3.30am in order to be on time for the cream carrier, who started his rounds very early.

How I loved walking out of the Convent gates in the crisp early morning before the dew. As the gates opened I would feel this rush of pleasure. I felt free, like a bird leaving its cage. As a special treat for carrying out this duty, both my companion and I would be given an extra piece of fruit to eat on our way. It seemed to be given to us in a secretive fashion, so it always tasted particularly sweet, and made me feel special. That feeling enhanced my experience of freedom as I headed towards the town.

When we reached the post office, my companion and I would sit on the steps, enjoying the last of our special fruit treat, while we awaited the arrival of the cream carrier. Before it came into view, we would hear the roar of the engine and the rattling of the empty cream cans which announced its approach. They seemed particularly loud in the quietness of the early morning. My little friend would jump up excitedly, saying: "Here it comes". And we would both stand on tip toe staring down the street to catch the first glimpse of it. It would lumber into sight, like a friendly dragon, emitting smoke and steam, but full of warmth. The driver always seemed to have kindness etched into his face, and he would give us a big open smile and a "G'day girls, lovely morning", as he pulled to a stop, and my friend happily clambered aboard, already thinking of home. As they set off, both she and the driver would wave vigorously to me, and I would return their wave, before turning to head back to the Convent.

As I strolled slowly back towards the school I would really soak up the freshness of the morning, and the pleasure of my own company. I would hear the birds with their pretty songs calling to each other, and their songs seemed to soar and echo in the clear morning air. Occasionally I would pass someone astir in their front yard, who also seemed to be enjoying the newness of the day, and we would exchange a wave and a smile. The world just seemed to be so beautiful and fresh at that moment. Even now I notice that the walkers I pass in the early morning seem happier and friendlier than those I pass on my late afternoon walks. I suppose it is because the morning walkers have not yet experienced the pressures, or been knocked down by the avalanches, of the day.

The feelings of freedom emanating from my morning walk remind me of how I used to feel when we travelled around in a caravan before we lived in the little fibro house.

Dad was always coming up with new ideas about how to make a living in those late war years. The aftermath of his youthful injuries had kept him out of that particular conflict. He decided to become a travelling salesman of men's and women's clothing and other merchandise to the country folk of Central Queensland, and acquired a car and caravan for that purpose. He arranged agencies for various merchandisers, including a men's tailor, and a women's frock shop in Brisbane, and after learning how to measure up for suits and the like we set off with our samples and catalogues to tend to the needs of the farming people. We travelled around from town to town and farm to farm, usually timing our visits to a particular area to co-incide with an important upcoming social event, like a show, dance or race meeting, which would be advertised in advance in the country newspapers.

Having advertised our intended arrival in advance ourselves by newspaper advertisements and strategically placed brochures in the shop windows of a small town, we would call at one farm after another in the district, where we were generally well received and invited to park our caravan while Dad measured up the farmer, and his workers and neighbours for suits, working clothes or whatever they required. Mum would sell dresses, sequins and other bric-a-brac to the women. If anyone wanted a hair cut, Dad would oblige, whilst Mum would trim and set the women's hair for the ball or whatever the occasion happened to be.

For those hard working, isolated country women, it was a rare treat to be able to pore over lovely materials and beautiful catalogues in their own back-yards, and at the same time enjoy having their hair done and chat with eager anticipation about the coming event. You could see the pleasure and excitement in their faces, and they would respond by swamping us with hospitality. Home made cakes and biscuits would be produced, and a picnic atmosphere would surround our little caravan parked by the side of the road or at the back of the farm house, as nearby neighbours would be summoned to join in the excitement.

Mum and Dad seemed to enjoy this gipsy life, and so did my sister and I, not least because it kept us out of school. I particularly remember the feeling of freedom which I experienced awakening in the early morning to the sound of roosters crowing or cattle bellowing, and knowing immediately that I did not have to get ready for school. The day would be mine, to do almost as I pleased. I could go and watch the farmer milk his cows, or feed the pigs and calves, or help the farmer's wife cooking a pile of cakes and scones over a hot wood-fired stove, and enjoy licking the spoon afterwards. She would always leave a little of the cake mixture in the bowl for my sister and me (and her own children, with whom we would vie for the first lick) to enjoy.

I particularly enjoyed this care-free life because, even then, I knew it could not last, as I often heard Mum and Dad quietly discussing the need to get my sister and me back into school. They said we were becoming too wild, and needed a more settled routine, as well as some more education. I could have gone on like that forever, but like all good things it had to come to an end.

One day it happened. Dad announced at the meal table that he and mother had arranged for us to attend the Sisters of Mercy Convent, in Biloela, one of the many country towns through which we had passed, and where they had made friends with some people whose children attended the school as day pupils. It was the only boarding school in the district which our parents could afford, and they had no intention of giving up their nomadic lifestyle yet, as they were enjoying it. Besides, they had not yet found anything else to do.

I remember the sinking feeling in my stomach the day Mother started getting together and labelling our clothes for the boarding school. There were 3 pairs of this and 2 pairs of that and one of those, all carefully labelled with my name, and placed in a pile. As the pile grew higher my heart sank lower. I had never had so many items of clothing all at once, and had never needed to have my name on anything! But that feeling of emptiness was nothing like the feeling of utter abandonment I felt when I first set foot in the dormitory of the Convent where I found I would be sharing a room with 15 other girls, all strangers to me except my sister! Looking back, I am amazed at how quickly that feeling dissipated, and how I soon adapted to the ordered life of a Convent girl, where everything happened according to what time it was on what day of the week.

Although I thought we had settled in fairly quickly, I know that for some time the Nuns considered my sister and I quite untamed. For example, there was the time when the Convent routine was disrupted by our enjoyment of April Fool's Day. My sister thought it would be a good joke to tell cook that Mother Superior said there was to be a second mass that morning so there was no need to cook the early breakfast. My sister and I then hid and watched in amusement as the Nun's, dressed in their black habits, lined up for a breakfast which wasn't ready. The excitable cook went into a frenzy and when Mother Superior confronted her, she quickly pointed the finger at the "two new wild girls" as the source of her embarrassment.

The smiles soon disappeared from our faces when Mother Superior carpeted us and told us she didn't believe in April Fool's Day, and that we had "the devil" in us. For our sins we were condemned to do extra washing up duty, which was normally done by the boarders on a roster basis. The day pupils could also have lunch with the boarders during the week, so lunch-time wash-ups were bigger than at other times. My sister and I were given a week's lunch-time wash-up duty as punishment for our misbehaviour.

Well, the Nuns soon learned that it was a mistake to put my sister and me on wash-up duty at the same time. They constantly had to intervene in our squabbles, as we both preferred to wash up, rather than to dry, and it was a constant battle about whose turn it was to wash. One day, in particular, I remember, our squabble began with one of us throwing a cup full of dish-water on the other, and ended with me throwing the whole dish of dirty water over my sister, whose angry screams brought the Nuns running in to separate us. I remember one saying: "We'd better be sure not to put you two on lavatory duty together, the result could be disastrous".

"Lavatory duty" related to the changing of the sanitary pans in the toilets, which were earth closets situated in the back yard of the Convent behind the boarding house. The sanitary cart called to collect the waste only once a week, but that was not sufficient because of the number of boarders relative to the number of toilets. So each week the sanitary man would leave two pans for each toilet, one for immediate use and the other as a spare. Mid-way through the week, the full pan would have to be removed, capped, and replaced with the empty spare one. That was another job for the boarders, who were also required to sweep and hose out the toilet block. The full cans would have to be carried outside and lined up behind the toilet building. No doubt that Nun had a vivid mental picture of what would happen if my sister and I started fighting while carrying out a full sanitary pan!

Although my sister and I often fought, we also often stood up for each other, when occasion demanded. I remember one time, when we were having lunch in the dining room. The day pupil seated next to me said she didn't like whatever it was we had been served, so, as a hungry boarder, I said I would have it. Just as I reached out to take the food off her plate, one of the Nun's appeared at the end of the table and on seeing my action said, sarcastically:-

"Oh, we are starving this poor girl. We don't want her to tell the world she is being starved here. Bring her some more food!"

She then proceeded to bring more food from the kitchen and place it in front of me, with the command:-

"Come on, eat it all up, we won't have you starving!"

She then watched me, and kept urging me to eat more, as each extra mouthful began to stick in my throat. I was so humiliated, I began to cry, and said: "I feel sick".

With that, my sister (who had been watching the process very closely) jumped to her feet, hands on hips, and announced in a loud and aggressive voice:

"No one is going to make my sister eat this, if she doesn't want to. She's not eating it!"

The Nun could see she meant business, and would have a fight on her hands is she persisted. So, satisfied with having humiliated me, she took away the food.

Later in our stay at the Convent, after we had quietened down a little, one of my sister's assigned duties was to prepare the doses of Epsom Salts which the boarders were required to take every Saturday morning. In those days it was thought that everyone needed a good clean out at least once a week. Perhaps that explained why the toilet pans were always filled to overflowing! My sister developed the trick of putting just water in two tumblers, one for her and one for me, having whispered to me in advance to pull a face and pretend it was the real thing. We continued to do that every week until we left the boarding school and became day-pupils when Mum and Dad settled in the town and rented the little fibro house. I sometimes think we overacted with the face pulling and the gagging that we went on with, but none of the Nun's ever tweaked to our secret.

Just then I am startled by the telephone ringing beside my bed. It is my younger son, with the news that he will be arriving in Brisbane tomorrow afternoon with his fiancee and her little girl. I'd best get some sleep now, so I can be fresh in the morning to prepare for their visit.

Cynthia (with Tom and Cetress) on her wedding day.

Tom and Cetress's wedding.

Cetress and Cynthia on her wedding day.

Cynthia and Travis's wedding.

Cynthia and Travis's wedding.

Travis and Cynthia's wedding with Warren Howell (best man) and Lola Harris (bridesmaid) at Biloela.

Ruth and Eddie Lindenmayer (Travis's parents) wedding.

Tom and Cetress's 50th wedding anniversary.

Travis and Cynthia's wedding.

Cynthia with Brad and Chris.

Tom and Cetress, Syliva and Cynthia.

Cynthia and Travis's wedding.

Tom Collins and Tom Brennan timber cutting.

Kids at play in creek at Lucknow Stud.

Brad and Chris.

Travis aged 6 months.

The Generations Relay

Tonight, as I go to bed, I don't feel like picking up my pen to start writing. But it's like my daily walk: I often don't feel like that either, but there is this deep down compulsion to exercise, and my nightly writing has become a similar sort of obsession. I know that if I don't do it, I won't be able to sleep because the random thoughts that I would have written down will go round and round in my head, like a merry-go-round. It has been such a happy few days that it is tempting to just nestle down into my pillow and re-live the pleasures of the week, but the writing bug is nibbling away at me and won't let me off that easily.

My younger son and his fiancée, with her delightful little daughter Elly, have been spending some time with me. Christopher and Polly seem so much in love, that their happiness is contagious, and little Elly's laughter and prattle have brought a brightness and a sparkle to the house reminiscent of when my boys were very young. It doesn't seem that long ago that they were only that age!

It's hard to let go the feeling that your children are your babies, but when you see them coming towards you it suddenly hits you, in an unguarded moment, that they are now mature young men. You sometimes wish you could do your mothering all over again, and fix up all your mistakes, but parenting is not like obtaining a driver's licence, where you just keep trying until you get it right. Rather, you just blunder on from one mistake to the next, hoping that in between you get enough right to point them in the right direction. But at this moment I am bent on selecting some good memories from the filing cabinet in my head, and not dwelling on what I could or should have done differently.

One of my good memories, which was stirred by young Elly's delight at my jumping rabbit trick with a rolled up handkerchief, was of Christopher's 5th birthday party. I had invited a dozen or so of his little friends from the neighbourhood and from kindergarten to attend for an afternoon of cake, cordial and games. Foolishly, I had decided to give each of his guests a little bag of surprises, which included a water pistol! Before long, I had a dozen 5 and 6 year olds running around the house squirting each other with water, and to top it all off it started to rain. You can imagine the chaos. Half wet children running in and out of the house, squealing with delight, while my husband and I tried to quieten them. At the same time I said to myself, "God, how could I have been so stupid". I was getting desperate for something to distract them when I remembered that my father, on a recent trip to Brisbane, had introduced me to an old barbering friend, Joe, who was an amateur magician. He had jokingly said to give him a call if I ever needed a magician, and I certainly needed one at that moment! So I gave Joe a call.

"Joe, I hope you're not busy" I begged, "but I'm desperate. I'm giving Chris a birthday party, and, as you can see, its raining. You wouldn't believe it, but I gave every kid a water pistol, and what with those and the rain, they're slipping and sliding all over the place. They're having a whale of a time, but if it keeps up I'll be sending some kids home with broken bones. Can you help me, please Joe?"

"No worries, love" he replied. "I've got a few tricks up my sleeve for kids of that age. I'll be round in under half an hour."

"God bless you, Joe" I responded, thankfully.

In no time he arrived, complete with magicians props (including some doves and a white rabbit). With promise of magic, we were able to settle the children in our garage where Joe proceeded to amuse and enthral an audience of wide-eyed, awe-struck youngsters, who were so quiet you could hear a pin drop, and I was able to mop up the results of their earlier excitement.

Christopher was so impressed by Joe's magic tricks that he immediately wanted to become a magician himself, and we had to buy him a magic set, with which he amused us and his friends for a number of years, as he practised and learned new tricks to add to his repertoire. I can still see the look of wonder on Chris's face as Joe pulled the white rabbit out of the black top hat, that rainy afternoon, and I can hear his childish laughter when the rabbit started hopping across the garage floor towards him and his mates. He still has an infectious laugh, and a slightly wacky sense of humour. In that, I think he takes after his grandmother, my mother. I have seen and heard them share a joke many times, and the picture of them both falling about with laughter, and hugging each other with the joy of shared amusement at one of Mum's tall stories (more fantasy than reality) of a past exploit, is a memory which I cherish.

When my older son, Brad, and his girlfriend, Adele, came to see Chris and Polly, and I looked at this large, powerfully built confident man in his mid-thirties, I could hardly conceive that he was the same person as the little boy with a school bag on his back whom I can remember running along the footpath of our street towards me one afternoon during his first year at school.

"Mum. Mum." He cried as he ran towards me as fast as his little legs would carry him, with his school bag bouncing up and down on his back. As he ran, he was pointing wildly towards a truck driving by, with a large black dog on the back. "They've stolen Judy. They've stolen Judy" he cried, pointing at the dog on the truck. As I followed his gaze, I too, for a moment, thought the black dog was my parent's "Judy", who was visiting us, with them, at that time. But my adult brain immediately realized it was not Judy, because I had just this minute passed her asleep on the verandah of our house. But Brad, who was on his way home from school, did not know that, and with his child's perception that there was only one beautiful black Labrador/Collie cross in the world, and that was Judy, he was heart broken to see her being driven away from near his home on the back of a truck, and concluded that these men must have stolen her.

"It's not Judy, Brad. It's just another dog like her", I offered, reassuringly.

"It's not! It's not! It's Judy!" Brad insisted, with a note of panic in his voice. "Where are they taking her?"

As we neared our front gate I could see that words alone would not satisfy him, so I called: "Here Judy", and Judy came lumbering down from the verandah, with her jowls and belly rolling from side to side, to greet us, and to lick the tears from Brad's face with her excitement. How the look of anguish on his face then turned to sheer joy, I shall always remember.

That thought brings a tear to my eye, as I remember that the last time I saw that sad look on Brad's face was when he came with us a few weeks ago to visit my father in the old folks home. He had bought a small portable radio for his grandfather, which he unpacked for him to explain its operation. As he did so, with his arm around his grandfather, he said:

"See Tom, you can listen to the news or the races or whatever you want to. Just switch it on, and turn this knob to tune it to the station you want."

"Thanks mate", said Dad, "but you'd better take it home with you. I won't be here long, and it will be something extra for me to pack up to take home."

It was then that Brad got that sad look, for he realized that his grandfather did not want to give a feeling of permanence to his surroundings by filling his room with personal items, yet we all knew that he would never come home to live again, and that this was to be his home for the rest of his days. Perceiving his grandfather's feelings, Brad responded (sadly)

"OK, Tom, I'll keep it for you until you come home."

That seemed to satisfy Dad, but he kept looking at Brad with a half puzzled look on his face, as if to say: "Who is this strange young man who wants to give me a radio?" Earlier I had said to him: "Dad, this is your grandson, Brad. Do you remember?" (Dad and Brad has always got on well. They seemed to have many common characteristics.) But now Dad just looked at him, and said quietly, "No, I don't remember. But he seems a nice young fella".

Brad, like all Dad's grand-children and (later) great-grandchildren always called him "Tom". That was Dad's choice. He insisted on it from the start, because he could not abide being called "Grand-father" or "Grand-Pa", since he didn't feel old enough to be a grand-father and, besides, he regarded "Tom" as a much friendlier form of greeting. Looking at him now, it's sad to think that he looks every one of his 88 years, and all the fight which he had in him as a young man has now gone out of him. And fight there certainly was in him, a-plenty.

I remember one particular occasion before we moved into the little rented fibro house, when Dad displayed his fighting qualities in a way which worked to our advantage (which was not always the case). At the time he had not long been operating the barber shop and adjoining billiard room in the small country town which became our home. In those early post-war years, accommodation was very difficult to obtain, and while we were waiting for the little fibro house (the only rental property in the town at that time) to become vacant, Mum, Dad, my sister and I were obliged to take up residence in the local hotel, an expensive exercise which Dad could not really afford. In order to try to reduce our living expenses, Dad prevailed upon the owner of the building which he leased for the barber shop-billiard saloon to build a small extension onto an existing shed, at the rear of the building to provide temporary accommodation for the family. Although plans were submitted to the local council for the work, under pressure from Dad, and thinking that approval was a mere formality, the owner undertook the work before the plans were approved, and we immediately moved into occupation of the building, which consisted of a kitchen, one bedroom and an enclosed verandah (where my sister and I slept).

Within days the local council met and, incensed that the work had been completed without its approval, rejected the building application and issued a notice requiring the removal of the illegal structure within 28 days. When the building owner presented Dad with the notice, and at the same time indicated that he did not wish to evict us or remove the structure, Dad said:

"Well, that suits me, because we're not shifting, and if the Council wants to make an issue of this, they'll have a fight on their hands."

In due course, the Council served a notice on Dad of its intention to demolish the "unlawful structure" on a named date, and requiring us to vacate it by that date. We sat tight. Dad's "Irish" was up, and there was no way he would go quietly.

When the appointed day arrived, the local building inspector (a small, ferret faced man) turned up on our door step and told Dad that we had until 2pm to remove our belongings, otherwise Council employees would remove them before carrying out the demolition work.

"I'd like to see them try" fumed Dad. "You can rest assured I'll be waiting for you, and you'll get a nice warm welcome too" he growled, at the same time giving him a look that would curdle milk.

The building inspector gave him an uncertain look in return, and departed in haste. Father immediately set about making preparations for their return. Firstly, he grabbed a handful of 4 inch nails and a hammer, and nailed every piece of our shabby furniture either to the floor or the wall of the building. Then he said to Mum:

"Fill a couple of those kerosene tins, Cetress, and boil all the water you can. Any bastard who tries to get in here will run out like a scalded chook!" And turning to my sister and I, he said: "It's your job to keep the wood up to the stove for your mother. Don't let me down now, or we'll all be out on the street."

As "zero hour" approached, Dad took up his position, full frame, on the landing leading from the billiard saloon to our quarters, and stationed Mum at the only other entrance, which was at the door to the verandah. Each was armed with a pot of near boiling water to be used only if a council employee crossed the imaginary lines, one at the entrance to the landing from the billiard saloon and the other at the top of the back stairs.

Just after 2pm the building inspector drove into the back yard, near the stairs to the verandah, but stayed seated in his ute. At the same time, the council foreman (a large, florid faced man) approached Dad's position on the landing, through the billiard saloon, followed closely by the local police constable, who stood back as an observer, ready to intervene only in the event of violence erupting.

The foreman glared at Dad, eyeball to eyeball, and demanded:

"Move yourself and the family, Tom, or it'll be the worse for you."

Dad glared back, and the high colour in his face, and his clenched jaw signalled his determination.

"It'll take a better man than you to put my wife and kids out on the street" said Dad, and he shouted over his shoulder, to my sister and I who were on duty in the kitchen "Keep the wood up to that fire girls, we'll need plenty of boiling water to scald these mongrels if they try to set foot in our home."

"What's happening out there, Cetress" he called to my mother.

"All quiet Tom, the dingo's still in his car" replied Mum.

"Well, what are you waiting for?" said Dad to the foreman "Come on if you're game," at the same time lifting his pot of water menacingly.

After a few more threats and curses, the foreman turned on his heel, gave a shrug, and stalked off saying: "I don't get paid enough for this shit", followed by the police constable who was wearing a slight grin.

Dad immediately dashed to join Mum at the other door, shouting,

"That's got rid of those mongrels, now for this one."

As he appeared at the doorway, the building inspector started up his ute and withdrew quickly from the scene. Thus ended the battle of the billiard room. The council decided to let sleeping dogs lie, for the time being, and waited until we moved out into the fibro house a couple of months later before carrying out their demolition.

The events of that day had been re-lived in my memory as Brad and Mum and I said good-bye to Dad at the old folks home, and we left this frail old man sitting in his wheel-chair looking after us with bewilderment on his face. Once again, Mum cried, "Why does it have to end like this" as Brad put his arm around her to comfort her.

My thoughts are now interrupted by the telephone ringing beside my bed. It is Chris to say they have all arrived home safely. That brings my thoughts back to their departure earlier today. Although it had been such a happy day, I could not avoid a flow of tears as I hugged Chris, Polly and Elly as they were about to enter the taxi which would take them to the airport. As Chris hugged me, he saw my tears and said "Don't cry, Mummy, I love you, and we'll see you again soon". In that instant I had this eerie feeling that I was my mother, who so often cried at my departure, and Chris was repeating what I had so often said to her. That made me realize that I am the next generation in line, and I had this crazy thought that I won't be around to protect my children when it is their turn.

That prompts me to rise to have my cup of chamomile tea to break the cycle of crazy thoughts and help me get off to a restful sleep. As I start to drift off I think: "It's time to liven this story up with a bit of romance". Tomorrow night, my early love life.

Brad, Travis and Chris,
Lone Pine, circa 1968.

Cynthia and Chris, circa 1973.

Cynthia with elder son Brad, 1963.

Cynthia, Brad and Chris, circa 1970.

Chris and Polly's wedding.

Travis, Brad and Adele.

On the Fringe of a New Life

Tonight I dawdle, as I shower, and dress myself for bed. Then, at last, as I slip between the sheets, I look at my beside table where I see the pen and paper, which have become my constant companions these last weeks, whilst my husband has been away. I'm finding it hard to get started with my writing tonight, and I decide to call my sister on the telephone, even though I know I am just giving myself an excuse to put off beginning my nightly chore for a few more minutes. I need inspiration, and none has come to me yet.

My sister and I, after all these years, still have our sibling disagreements. Something I mention about life in the city prompts her to say to me:

"You're lucky. Dad let you go to Brisbane. He wouldn't let me go, and I've been stuck in this dead-end place all my life!"

"How many times, do I have to tell you", I reply, "Dad didn't let me go, I just went. You could have gone too if you'd wanted. There was nothing to stop you."

After I finish talking to her, my mind drifts back to how it was I came to live in the city, a thing I had often said I would never do. But it's amazing what love can make you do.

I remember how Dad always made the decisions in our family, and just announced what was going to happen, without any discussion. On one such occasion, as he sat at the head of the table, he announced that he had put his name in a land ballot, but did not expect to win a block, as there were only 14 available, and many more applicants. But if he did, he explained, we would be starting from scratch, as the blocks were all undeveloped Brigalow scrub. I marvelled at how Mum just accepted this prospect without batting an eye. She always went along with Dad's adventures without question. I, however, didn't welcome the news. I was just at the age where I was beginning to enjoy life in town, with my boyfriend, and the movies and the dances to go to.

Needless to say, in a few months time, when the result of the ballot was announced, Dad had drawn a block about 30 miles out of Biloela, where we then lived. So the house, and Mum's hairdressing business were put on the market, and Mum and Dad began to make preparations for their next adventure. They asked me was I going to come with them, or if not what my plans were. I told them I wanted to stay in town, and would go and live with my sister and her husband and child, in the house next door.

Mum said, "You've got that engagement ring sitting in your glory box, you've had plenty of time to think about it. Now would be a good time to announce your engagement. He's such a nice boy, you wouldn't want for anything. I don't know why you keep putting it off."

I replied: "Don't push me Mum. I'll do it if and when I want to. I don't feel right about it."

"I give up" she said, "I don't know what on earth you want. One of these days girl you'll look around and he'll be gone. There are plenty of other fish in the sea!"

My boyfriend had presented the engagement ring a few months before, but I said, "Wait a while, I'm not ready yet" and I pushed it in among the towels in my glory box and tried to forget about it. I just couldn't bring myself to put it on, I'm not sure why, but I also hadn't completely rejected the idea that I might marry him one day.

In due course, Mum and Dad packed up and moved out to the land, which they had just cleared, and I moved in with my sister. I got a job with the nice lady who ran the Dairy Queen Ice Cream Parlour and coffee shop in the town. She and her husband were always talking about their two sons, who were both in Brisbane, the older one studying to be a pilot, and the younger studying law at the University. From the way they described them I realized their sons were the two new boys in town whom I and some girl friends had seen through Mum's shop window, not so long before.

It was not long after I took that job that my romance with the farmer boy came to an end. It just fizzled out. I think he got tired of waiting for me to make up my mind, and started looking elsewhere.

With Mum and Dad out on their land, I was thrown into a different environment with my sister and her family, and missed the familiarity of my room in the house which had become so comfortable over the past few years. Although it was busy at work most of the time, there was a quiet period on Wednesday and Saturday nights, (when we stayed open late to cater for the movie crowd) while we would be waiting for the interval rush to start. During those quiet periods I felt very lonely, having just seen other young couples going off to the movies together, including (on some occasions) my former boy-friend and his new girl. I sometimes wondered if I had done the right thing by not becoming engaged to him after all.

A couple of weeks later, the people who ran the shop began showing excitement as their younger son was soon due to arrive home on holidays. After his arrival, we were introduced, and he soon began to come down almost daily to help in the shop. At first I was a little embarrassed, because I wondered if he would remember that I had asked him to sit me down during our one and only dance on his first visit to town some months before. If he did remember, he gave no sign of it, and my early shyness soon passed. Sometimes, as we worked together, I would sneak a sly peek at him out of the corner of my eye, as I did think he was quite cute. Once or twice I thought I caught him giving me a sly look at the same moment, but I didn't dwell on the thought. Although I remembered thinking, as he had placed his cheek to mine that time at the dance, that he must have babies all over Brisbane, the talk I had heard from his parents in the mean-time made me wonder if he had ever even kissed a girl, as they painted him as pure as the driven snow.

On the home front at my sister's place, things were always in chaos. Her husband, who was a truck owner-operator had some time previously brought home a young orphaned donkey, which he had picked up off the road when its mother was accidentally killed. It grew up like a member of the family, and walked in and out of the house like a pet dog. We of course called him "Francis" after the talking mule in the Donald O'Connor movies. Francis and Whiskey, my dog, became great mates, and my nephew, who was 3 or 4 years old, was the constant companion of them both.

Sometimes Francis would follow me to work, as I always walked down the street from home. When that happened, the garage boys on the corner would give me a ribbing, whistling and calling out things like: "Which twin has the Toni [The "Toni" was a very popular home permanent process at that time, which was widely advertised by the depiction of a pair of twin girls, each displaying a beautiful head of curls, over a caption which read: "One twin has an expensive professional perm, and one has the Toni home perm. Which Twin has the Toni?" and, of course, you couldn't tell the difference between them.] When I got to the shop on those days, I would give Francis an ice cream, which he would eat with relish, before strolling off home.

One morning, when Francis was eating his ice cream out of my hand, I looked up and there was the boss's son, (Travis), smiling at me with an interested look on his face.

"Would you like to go to the movies with me tonight?' he said. "We have to help Mum at interval, anyway, and take her home after the movies."

"OK" I said, and so it was arranged.

He picked me up that night in his father's black Customline sedan, after dropping his mother at the shop. In those days, the movies were always preceded by the playing of the National Anthem ["God Save the Queen"] for which the audience always stood. As the Anthem ended, and we began to sit for the movies, his soft hand wrapped itself around mine, and instantly it seemed so natural that it felt as if we had known each other for ages. With no words spoken, we both accepted that from that moment we were “an item”.

After the movies, we picked up his mother from the shop to drive her home. She handed me some sandwiches which she had made for my brother-in-law to take with him out on the road the next day. I couldn’t wait to get her home so I could have her son to myself on the drive to my place. When we did arrive outside my sister’s home, we couldn’t wait to get at each other, and immediately fell to passionate kissing in the front seat. At that very moment I felt a nudge on my back through the open window of the car. It was Francis, welcoming me home. He was demanding attention. Somehow, in between kisses, I managed to open the packet of sandwiches and slip one to Francis, who ate it greedily, just as I was greedily devouring Travis’s kisses. Francis kept coming back for more, and so did I. As the sandwiches tasted sweet to Francis, so the kisses tasted sweet to me. Travis too was so intent upon and lost in our kisses that he did not seem to notice me feeding the sandwiches to Francis, or if he did he didn’t care.

At last we drew breath and, as difficult as it was, dragged ourselves apart. We both knew his mother would be worried about what had become of him, and besides it was our first encounter, and we were probably both a little stunned by the suddenness of it. However, we quickly made an arrangement to meet the next day (Sunday) for an outing in the car, which he was sure he could borrow while his father was at bowls and his mother at the shop.

I couldn’t wait for the next afternoon to arrive, and all that morning I was in a muddle. My sister’s house was even more chaotic than usual. Francis and Whiskey were in and out of the house, followed by my young nephew, who had just learned how to play his favourite record, “Woody The Woodpecker”, on his mother’s radiogram, which he played over, and over again, at maximum volume. All you could hear through the house was:

“Ah, ha, ha, ha, ha; Ah, ha, ha, ha, ha. That’s the Woody Wood Pecker song”, and my sister shouting at him to “Turn that thing down!”

As if things weren’t chaotic enough, Francis tried to eat the neighbours wet clothes off the line, and managed to dislodge the prop (which was used to raise the single clothes line which every house had stretched across the back yard in those pre-Hill's Hoist days) bringing all the washing crashing down into the dirt and the bindiis. The neighbour, faced with the prospect of having to re-do her whole wash, by hand, with only the assistance of a copper boiler and a hand-wringer, was furious.

"That bloody donkey is nothing but a pest. It shouldn't be allowed in town. I should report you to the Council," she shouted at my sister.

"What makes you so sure it was my Francis" cried my sister, who was in complete denial, "It might 'ave been the wind, or those bloody kids of yours. Anyway, tell your kids to stop calling Francis into your yard."

Just then, when the chaos was at its peak, in walked my date for the day. He was early, and I wasn't ready! He would learn, in time, that I was seldom on time, just as I would learn that he was always early. In a rush, now, I headed for the bathroom to take a shower, at the same time throwing him my frock and pointing in the direction of the ironing board.

"Here, you can iron this, if you like, while I have a shower" I said, and disappeared into the bathroom without waiting for an answer.

When I emerged, in my bath robe, to find him struggling with my frock on the ironing board, iron in hand, I realized that he had probably never used an iron before, or at least not to iron a woman's frock. So I quickly grabbed up the frock and threw it on in haste to get him away from this mad house. We disappeared down the street to the strains of "Woody the Woodpecker" and of Francis bidding me good-bye with his loud "Hee-Haw, Hee-Haw". As we turned the corner out of our street, Travis started laughing so hard he could hardly drive. "I've never had a welcome and departure quite like that before" he said between laughs, but he would soon discover that such goings on were the norm in our household.

We drove aimlessly out of town, with no particular destination in mind, turning this way and that up various quiet country lanes, past fields of lucerne and sorghum, and small groups of cattle sheltering from the sun under the clumps of trees which farmers left standing for just that purpose. Neither of us paid much attention to the scenery, we only had eyes and thoughts for each other. At last we came to a quiet, cool, shady lane, where Travis brought the big Customline to a halt. Hardly had he pulled on the handbrake and turned off the ignition than we were in each others arms enjoying once more the rush of youthful hormones which came the moment our lips met. After a few minutes of wild passion, the closeness of the steering wheel and the dash board became a hindrance and, almost in unison, we tumbled over the back of the seat into the rear compartment, where we became involved in a marathon of kissing that whittled the afternoon away. To us, lost in our hunger for each other, time seemed to stand still. We were mindless of the climbing temperature inside the black car standing still on that summer afternoon, and of the sweat which ran down our faces and mingled with out kisses, as we writhed and wriggled to get into more comfortable positions to continue our frantic "necking". From time to time we did pause, only to catch our breath (or to open the car's doors to catch the passing breeze) before diving back into it again.

Before we realized it, the sun had gone down, and it was getting dark. With the setting sun our passion cooled just enough for us to take a break from love-making. We again drove aimlessly around the country-side, just enjoying the closeness of each other and the quiet companionship in which neither of us felt the need to talk. At one point we stopped beside a night tennis court in another small country town, and kissed each other more gently, but repeatedly, while the players on court continued their game, oblivious to our presence.

Suddenly, Travis sat up and looked at his watch for the first time since we had left my sister's home early that afternoon. "Hell!" he said "It's eight o'clock. I was supposed to pick up Mum from the shop at 6 o'clock. She'll be worried sick. We'd best head home as quick as we can."

As he swung the big car towards home, and stood on the accelerator for more speed, I looked down at my crushed dress, and wondered why I had bothered asking him to iron it earlier! I dreaded what his mother would say, but I still enjoyed snuggling into him and the time it took to reach home. We decided that he should drop me off at home before going to face his mother, because one look at my crushed dress and whisker reddened face would have told her that we had not spent the afternoon sight-seeing! But the moment we pulled up outside my sister's place, we both fell off cloud 9 with a thud. My sister was looking out for us, and came straight to the car, where she said to Travis:

"You're in big trouble. You'd better scoot down to your mother's straight away. They've had the search party out looking for you. I tried to say you would be OK, and just out driving around, but they insisted something must be wrong. You are always so reliable and on time."

My brother-in-law, who was standing back laughing, then said:

"I tried to tell them not to expect perfection, he was with you, after all, but they insisted that he is always on time and never let them down, so they imagined the worst."

As I got out of the car, and bolted for the front door, my brother-in-law kept laughing and teasing me, saying: "I wouldn't be game to go back there to work tomorrow! And by the way, that boss of yours is pretty bloody lousy. I didn't get many sandwiches for my money." At that moment I felt a flash of guilt, but Francis and I were both in enough trouble already, and I wasn't going to make it worse by owning up to what I had done with his sandwiches.

Travis later told me that when he sheepishly confronted his parents that night, they were so pleased to see him alive and well they didn't ask too many embarrassing questions about why he was so late. He mumbled something about trouble with the car and that his watch must have stopped, and then listened patiently as they described their frantic searches, which included a visit to the local swimming holes to shine torches into the water looking for us. At one point, one of the searchers had raised a false alarm when he called out that he thought he saw the car's tail light in the creek, and Travis's father went as pale as a ghost and almost passed out.

Next day, when I fronted at the shop, I was most apprehensive about the reception I would receive. Travis's father, being the big cuddly bear he is, just grinned at me, gave me a hug, and said: "Honey, you took 10 years off my life, but its still good to see you." His mother was a little cooler, and took some time to thaw out, but it was soon forgotten, and life returned to normal, except that it would never be the same for me, because I was now head over heels in love.

The next couple of weeks just flew by, as Travis and I fell deeper and deeper in love. We were almost constantly in each other's company, and treasured each moment because the time for him to return to his studies in Brisbane was fast approaching, and we both dreaded that day's arrival. But arrive it did. On the morning of his departure, he came around to my house to say good-bye. I remember how we clung to each other, and how the tears flowed and mingled with our kisses, making them taste salty. At last he had to go, and as he dragged himself away, and then turned to wave good-bye, my heart sank, and I felt as if part of me had been ripped out.

Remembrance of that lonely, empty feeling, brings me back to the present. That youthful boy, who became my husband, is now away on one of his longer work-related absences. I still miss him. He is nearing his retirement, and his light brown hair has turned to silver (as, too, would have much of mine, but for the hairdresser's magic bottle). But I know that when I look out of our window, and see him walking down the path to our front door on his return, to me he will still be that young boy I saw through my mother's shop window all those years ago, and I will still feel like the young girl who saw him.

Those happy memories and pleasant anticipation help me to drift into a peaceful sleep. Tomorrow night I will write about how I followed my love to the city.

Breaking Away

As I take up my pen tonight, I am eager to begin, because I have a warm feeling in my chest from the memory of my early romance with Travis, which I wrote about last night. That memory stayed with me all day, and I can't wait to enjoy the reminiscence of those special feelings again.

The memories are not entirely painless, because I also remember how lonely I felt when he returned to Brisbane at the end of that first heady summer of our newfound love. After he returned there we wrote those poignant love letters to each other which young lovers did in those days when they were apart. I still have them in my bottom drawer, tied up in a piece of ribbon. I guess if the telephone had been as available then as it is today, I wouldn't have those tangible reminders of that bitter-sweet time. Very few people had a telephone in their homes in those days, and even those who did seldom made trunk calls half-way across the State. It was too expensive, and besides, we were so used to writing letters that that is just what we did. It really didn't occur to us to use the telephone as we do now. The art of private letter writing is dying, with the advances of technology through the telephone, and the mobile phone to e-mail and the Internet.

During our enforced separation I would mark off the days on the calendar, counting the time until my lover's next holiday period, when we could be together again. In that period I was thankful for a few special friends, especially some older ones who would stroll over to the shop where I was working and pass the quiet times with me, over a cup of coffee, by telling me stories about their lives. As there was no T.V. in Queensland in those days, people did communicate more with each other. If they got bored at home the women would take their knitting or fancy-work and pop in next door or to a friend down the street for a chat and a cup of tea. Some of the men would go down to the club or the pub for a beer, or just stroll down the street to see who they might run into and share a few yarns with to pass the time. Now, when I revisit that small country town, I find that you could fire a cannon down the main street at 9 o'clock most nights and not hit a soul. Most of them are at home watching the T.V.

I feel lucky that I was able to spend some quiet hours listening to the likes of "Nugget", the grizzled yardman from one of the pubs, who had been in Changi, and had seen a kind of life I couldn't even imagine, or Father Tom, the local Catholic priest, who liked a fag and a bet on the horses, and a yarn.

"Nuggett", for all he had been through, was a gentleman still. He would tip his hat (which he always wore) to any woman he passed on the street, and always had a kind word for young ones, like me. I can still remember him bringing over his little tin of treasures to show me. It contained old faded and crushed photographs of some of the mates he lost in Changi, and letters he had received before being captured which he had managed to keep hidden and preserved, at great risk, through those terrible years. He, and most of the other old timers I used to yarn with in those days, who seemed to sense my need for company, have long since finished their life's journey, and I am glad I had the opportunity to travel part of that journey with them.

Recently on a visit to my father in the old folks home I saw a face I barely recognized, until Mum told me who it was. He was just lying there babbling in-coherently, and staring sightlessly into space. When Mum told me who he was, and I remembered how he used to pass the time with me all those years ago, I sat with him for a moment, and squeezed his old wrinkled hand, and was able to recall how strong those hands used to be and how his now sightless eyes would light up when he told one of his tall stories.

Driving Mum home from that visit to father, I remember we

drove past the spot where the Dairy Queen shop used to be. Like so many of the old timers, it too has gone into history. But passing the spot reminded me of how I stood there, in the shop, all those years ago, waiting impatiently for Travis's father to bring him back from the airport on his next arrival on holidays. I remember re-combing my hair and re-doing my lipstick, over and over, as I anxiously awaited his arrival. Would he have changed? Would he still feel the same about me? Doubts filled my head, until our eyes met. The spark was still there, and the kisses still full of fire. But as happy as the re-union was, we knew it would soon be followed by another unbearable parting. It was then we decided that I would have to move to the city to be with him, although that was something I had thought I would never do.

Having made that decision, I had to break the news to Mum and Dad. For that purpose I travelled out to their farm on the following weekend. At first when I told them, I didn't get much reaction. I think it took a couple of days for it to sink in that I was serious, and not just fantasising. A few days after I had returned to town, Dad made a special trip in to see me, saying he wanted to have "a chat about your plans". We drove up to the show grounds, where he parked the car.

"I don't like the idea of you going to the city", he said. "You don't know what trouble you could get in down there. You're only going to chase that bloke, and if he dumps you, which is well on the cards, you'll be stranded there, a target for every no-hoper around the place and a great worry to your mother and I. Besides, they have just shut down the prostitute houses, and the place is rife with disease, and you never know what you night catch."

"No Dad", I said, "Travis is really nice, and he'll look after me. He is going to be a barrister one day." I thought that would impress him, but no.

"Those mongrels!" he replied. "They'll only swear your life away! They're just parasites. We don't need 'em. All you need is honesty, a good hand-shake, and a punch in the nose for anyone who breaks his word, not all those law cases."

I sat through Dad's tirade in silence, as I always did. He thought he had talked me around, but he should have known from past experience that my silence did not mean agreement. Dad could never quite come to grips with the fact that, unlike my sister, I would just weather his outbursts in silence, and then go ahead and do my own thing, whether he approved or not. He always called me a fish out of water, and often said: "I don't know what to do with that girl."

He went back to the farm, thinking he had talked me around, and I went on with my plans to leave.

Travis and I didn't realize that what seemed so right for us didn't seem right to others, so there was more resistance to come.

There were two travelling salesmen who had been regularly coming to town for several years who had become firm friends with Mum and Dad, and who had also recently become friends with Travis's parents. They became worried that Travis and I were complete opposites, and that our relationship would end in disaster if I followed him to the city. So they took it upon themselves to have a "heart to heart" talk with me, and dropped into the shop at a quiet time for a cup of coffee. We had always had an easy relationship, and at the start I was cracking my usual jokes and running off at the mouth about all kinds of nonsense. But soon they became serious, and started telling me that they were worried my relationship with Travis wouldn't work.

"You come from two different worlds" one said.

"Silly me" I replied "I always thought there was only one world, and we're all in it together."

"Be serious" said the second. "There's the education gap, for a start. He's at University and you've just had a quick brush through a few schools here and there as your parents followed their gipsy life around the country-side. You'll have to go up to his level, which I can't see you doing, or he'll end up coming down to yours, which would be a shame. If he has to give up his study, he'll regret it and resent you for the rest of his life."

By this time, my self-esteem was taking a battering, and with their constant harping I decided that I would try to show a sensible side.

The only way I could think to do that was to become quieter and more reserved. So from then on, whenever they came to the shop (as they did practically every day they were in town) instead of rabbiting on in my usual fashion, I would be quiet, polite, and sensible, thinking that they would be pleased that I had taken notice of them. Instead, it back-fired, and they started pestering me about what was the matter, as I was not myself. My pride wouldn't let me say that I was trying to change, as they had been telling me I would need to, so I just kept saying "nothing" in response to their enquiries.

One night, after I arrived home at my sister's place at the end of my shift, I found them both there waiting for me. They had been due to move on to the next town that night, but said they had decided to stay on to get to the bottom of my sudden quietness. They kept insisting that something must be wrong. "Come on, you can tell us anything" one insisted, with a concerned look on his face.

I don't know what made me say it (because in those days sex just wasn't discussed and pregnant unmarried girls were a disgrace who were usually sent away, either to have an illegal abortion or to be hidden in some "wayward" girls' home until their babies were born and quickly adopted out) but I stupidly said: "I'm pregnant." Well, that created a storm I hadn't bargained on.

"Good God, I knew it, but this is terrible" said the older of the two, "Tom will spread Travis around town like a pound of butter, and it will break his parent's hearts, because they've worked so hard to get him this far. Quick, pack your ports, we know of an abortionist in another town. We'll set it up for you: You don't have to worry about money or anything".

At this stage I began to panic, because I was unable to get a word in to explain that I was only joking, and that we hadn't even done the unmentionable act for me to get pregnant. My pride still wouldn't let me say that I was just following their advice and trying to change.

Eventually I did manage to convince them that I was not pregnant. They realized, then, that I hadn't really changed, but when they left they were still a bit miffed that my "game" had delayed their travel plans. I said to my sister: "The bloody idiots deserved that. Trouble is it backfired on me for a while."

About a week later, I boarded the plane for Brisbane, to start my new life in a "different world" as my traveller friends had called it. At that stage, I didn't realize how right they were, and what lay ahead. All I could think of was of my love waiting to collect me at the airport to take me to cloud nine again.

Tomorrow night I shall have a closer and more realistic look at "cloud nine".

Sylvia.

The Big Smoke

Tonight, as I prepare for bed, the sound of a departing aircraft overhead reminds me of the excitement I felt as I prepared to board another, much smaller, aircraft, all those years ago, to leave my country life behind for the big city. Just as I cried the other day when Chris was leaving, I remember how my Mum cried and said: "I'm going to be worried sick about you," as she hugged me and pressed her teary face against mine. "Your father reckons Brisbane is a big, dirty place full of crims and germs. You don't know anyone except that boy. What if he leaves you in the lurch?"

"Don't worry, Mum" I replied. "He'll look after me. If I get into trouble I can always go to Grand-Ma's. What's her address again." "That old bitch," said Mum. "She was never that nice to me, and she doesn't really like company. But anyway, she lives at Broadway Street, Carina, if you're really desperate. You'd better write that down." "That's alright Mum. I'll remember that. All the movie stars are on Broadway."

As I boarded the aircraft and waved Mum goodbye, all I could think about was my love waiting for me to arrive, and how I would soon be in his arms again. As the aircraft taxied towards take-off, and Mum faded into the distance, I didn't realize how much I would miss her, or how much my life was going to change.

As the aircraft, at last, began to descend towards Brisbane Airport, I experienced the first slight sinking feeling in my stomach, and I wondered whether it was just the sudden dipping of the aircraft's nose or a little fear of the unknown which caused it. Whatever it was, the feeling disappeared as I fell into the arms of my love waiting for me at the terminal gate. As we scrambled, then, amongst the crowd of people in the terminal to collect my bag and make our way to Travis' car (which he shared with his brother) I clung tight to him for fear of being separated from him and lost in the milling, unfamiliar crowd.

After a few more kisses and cuddles in the car park, we set off. Travis said we were going to St Lucia. I had no idea where that was. It seemed to take us forever to get there, passing through the city on the way. I was overwhelmed by the amount of traffic, the number of people, and the sheer size of the place. It reminded me of a swarm of bees all buzzing around a hive, and everything was all just a jumble to me. I thought, with a touch of panic, "I'll never find my way around this." I voiced that fear to Travis, who replied with confidence: "Don't worry, you'll soon get the hang of it, and I'll be around to show you the ropes."

"The first thing we have to do is find you a place to stay," he said. "Unfortunately, my Uni college is all male, and the female colleges are only for students. But there's a mixed hostel near the Uni which has a vacancy, and I thought we might have a look at that first. It's just down the road from my place."

That appealed immediately to me, because the closer I could be to him at that stage the more secure I felt. I also realized that he wouldn't always have the car available, since he had to share it with his brother who lived on the other side of town, and who had to travel out to Archerfield regularly for his flying lessons.

So our first stop was the St Lucia Hostel, where we were interviewed by the proprietor to see if I was suitable for admission to her establishment. After showing us the layout of the place, including the room which would be mine (if I was accepted), she took us to her apartment for the interview, saying there were some rules which we both needed to be aware of and agree to abide by before I could be admitted. She made it clear that breaches of her rules would not be tolerated. I remember sitting there with my back straight, knees together, hands in lap while she rattled off the rules, which included:

"No food in bedrooms."

"No wet towels left on beds."

"All residents to leave kitchen clean and tidy after use."

"All visitors out by 10pm."

"No members of the opposite sex, whether residents or guests, allowed in a resident's bedroom." "You may entertain one or two visitors up until 10pm in the common lounges," she said.

After that one, I didn't hear anymore, although she continued to rattle them off. The thought of not being able to cuddle Travis in the privacy of my room, after the relative freedom of living in my sister's house, was suffocating. But, having no other choices at that stage, we both agreed, although I secretly thought: "Rules are made to be broken." However, I had a feeling it would not be easy to get away with breaking them under her watchful eye. So I was accepted.

As Travis carried my port to my room (which seemed large compared to the room I had at my sister's place, yet still claustrophobic in atmosphere) I started to cry, and said: "I hate this place already," and felt like breaking one rule immediately by dragging him into the room, and closing the door so that we could be in our own little world again.

"Give it a chance" he said. "It mightn't be so bad when you get used to it. At least its not far away from my place, and not too expensive. You might make some friends here."

"I hate it, I hate it, I hate it," I replied. "I'll never like it. There are too many people. It looks and smells and sounds like a boarding school. And all those rules!" So saying, I tore up the printed copy of the "House Rules" which the proprietor had handed me.

With a bewildered look Travis took the pieces and put them in his pocket before I could throw them all around the hallway outside my room, as was my intention at the moment. With that, we decided to get out of the place for a while, and went driving around St Lucia and the University grounds, eventually parking by the river as night began to fall. There we clung to each other for a few hours, desperate to share as much time together as we could before the "rules" of his college and my hostel forced us apart.

That night, when I had to shower in the communal female bathroom amongst all those strange girls, who chatted away amongst themselves about things that were foreign to me, it really came home to me that what those two salesmen friends had said about "two different worlds" wasn't so silly after all. I now began to understand what they meant, and I would understand more over the coming weeks.

As I walked hurriedly from the bathroom towards my room, I had to pass through the lounge, which seemed crowded with residents chatting and laughing. I felt terribly self-conscious, so I scooted past as quickly as I could. However, in that brief moment, my eye caught that of a young Chinese boy in the group, with whom, strangely, I felt a degree of instant rapport. Perhaps it was that he, having been something of an outsider himself not long before, recognized another outsider immediately, and a small spark of compassion flashed from his eye to mine. Certainly, I felt slightly comforted by what I detected as the first small sign of acceptance by someone in this otherwise alien group.

The next morning, after a tearful, restless night, I delayed going to the kitchen to make a cup of tea, until I thought that most of the residents would have finished their breakfast and would have left to go about their day's activities.

As I poked my head timidly outside my door, I immediately saw the Chinese boy, and I said to him: "Have they all gone?" He said: "Yes, you'll be alright now. Come and have a cup of tea in the kitchen." I told him my name, and he told me his. I told him I had just arrived from the country, and this all seemed very strange to me. He said: "You'll get used to it. I did. I'll introduce you to some of them tonight."

At that moment, a girl came into the kitchen to have a cup of tea, followed by the cleaning lady. They started talking about how a couple had just been asked to leave because they had been caught kissing in the lounge. That was enough for me. I decided then and there I was not going to stay in this crazy, restrictive place any longer. So when Travis arrived, about an hour later, to take me out for the day and to show me the bus route into town and so on, there I was waiting with my port packed. The Chinese boy had carried it downstairs for me. He had tried to persuade me to stay, but I would not be swayed.

Travis looked a bit stunned when he saw me. Looking back, I realize that he was only 20, and it was a lot for him to cope with, but at the time I was caught up with my own efforts to cope with all that was happening to me.

"Where will we go?" he said. "I don't know" said I. "Just drive around. We might see something smaller that appeals to me."

Travis thought it might be better to look up the "Rooms to Let" advertisements in the paper, so we stopped at the nearest corner shop to buy a newspaper. We anxiously scanned the "Rooms to Let" column, and although there were many, we found only one which I thought might suit me. It had only 6 rooms, women only, with use of the kitchen and dining room, and share the bathroom. I thought I would not be daunted by a large crowd of strangers, as I had been at the Hostel.

The landlady at this establishment was a biggish Italian woman, without the brusque business-like way of the Hostel proprietor, and the place looked a bit more homely. It had been a large family home, re-modelled for a rooming house. But here, again, there were some rules, but not as many as in the other place. Still, the "no men in bedrooms" rule applied. That was the hardest rule for me to swallow. In this strange environment I needed Travis close to me all the time. It seemed that, despite following him to Brisbane, we were just as far apart as before. In those days "respectable" establishments couldn't allow young men and young women to be in a bedroom together, it would give the place a bad reputation.

One of the other residents, a young woman a few years older than me, introduced herself. My eyes were immediately drawn to a sore on her face, which was probably a simple cold sore, but at that stage Father's warnings about those "diseases" being rife in the city since the closure of the brothels came immediately to my mind. So I kept my distance.

That night, as I kissed Travis good night, lingeringly, in the car outside my new lodgings, I said to him: "Did you notice the sore on that woman's face? Do you think she's a street woman with that disease Father warned me about."

Travis laughed, and said: "Don't be silly, honey. You worry too much. You don't have to sleep with her!"

Despite his re-assurance, I went to my lonely room full of trepidation, wishing I could have kept him there with me. Again, I had a sleepless night. I found the bed had a sag in it like a sway-backed mule, which didn't help. Eventually, full of frustration, I pulled the mattress off onto the floor, where I spent the rest of the night sobbing into my pillow.

Next morning, I put on my red padded dressing-gown to go to the bathroom. I found that it had one of those gas geysers which you have to light to heat the water for bath or shower and I had no idea of how to operate it. The woman with the sore on her face explained it to me, but I didn't fully understand. I stood back from this monster, striking and throwing match after match at its open mouth until, all of a sudden, it exploded into life, and seemed to lurch towards me like an angry dragon breathing fire.

"Shit" I yelled, and sat on the floor with a thud, where I started to cry again. While I was crying, I noticed what appeared to be little white things on my naked body under the dressing gown. In hysterics, I picked one up to see if it would crack between my fingernails. I was sure it did. I screamed then. I was sure I had "the crabs" which Mum had told me to beware of in strange toilets.

The woman with the sore on her face poked her head in the door to enquire if I was alright, which only made me cry all the louder.

"Call me a cab please," I said. "I'm getting out of here" as I headed for my room.

She could see I was not in a state to be asked why.

Just then, the Italian landlady came waddling down the hallway, saying:

"Whats-a-matter you? Why you cry like a baby?"

I said: "I hate this city."

"Why?' she asked. "My grand-children only five, don't-a cry like-a that!"

There's nothing worse, as a grown-up than being told by another older grown-up that their five-year-old grandchild has got more composure than you. At that stage, I had no pride, and I cried even louder.

When the taxi arrived, I was still crying. The driver came to the door, and called out: "Who called for a cab?" The Italian lady pointed towards my room off the hallway and said: "Its-a-her. She cry like a baby."

He came to my door, and said: "Did you want a taxi, lady?"

"Yes," I said, between sobs. "Help me pack my clothes, I have to get out of here."

By now I had thrown on a dress, but the taxi driver had to help me throw the rest of my clothes into my port, while tripping over the mattress on the floor from time to time.

Eventually, we got to the taxi with my port, with me still crying, and the Italian lady still singing out from the front steps: "I don't know why she cry like a baby. Better you go somewhere else."

As I sat, still sobbing, in the front seat, the driver said: "Where to, luv?"

I said: "I don't know. Take me to Grand-Ma's."

"Where's Grand-Ma's?" he asked.

"I forget" said I. "She lives in a street with a Hollywood name."

"You'll have to give me a bit more of a clue than that, luv" he replied, "We pride ourselves on being able to find a needle in a haystack, but we have to know the general whereabouts of the haystack first!"

"I hate this Brisbane. I hate it. I hate it." I wailed.

After a few minutes, I remembered that Grand-Ma's street was Broadway Street, but not the suburb. The taxi-driver consulted his street directory, and said: "There's three Broadway streets. One at Carina, one at Redhill and one at the 'Gabba. Do you know which one?"

"Carina, I think" was my reply, through more sobs.

"OK," said the cabbie, "we'll give it a go," and off he set for Carina.

I sobbed all the way, still carrying my dressing gown, and the cabbie kept glancing at me with quite a sympathetic look on his face. Goodness knows what awful fate he thought he was rescuing me from.

Eventually, we turned into Broadway Street, Carina, and I was able to recognize my grandmother's house from the visits which I had made there, over the years, with Mum and Dad.

Grand-ma was surprised to see me but in the state I was in she couldn't turn me away. In fact, she was very kind, and took me into the kitchen, where she made me a nice cup of tea and helped dry up my tears.

"Maybe you should think of going back home", she suggested.

"I'm not ready to give up yet" I replied. "Besides, I don't want to give them the pleasure of saying: 'We knew you couldn't last long down there.'"

Grand-ma then showed me the little room at the back of her place which she said I could stay in for a while, until I got my bearings. I gratefully accepted. It was only as I settled into that room that I looked closely at my dressing-gown, which I had carried all the way, and noticed that what, in my panic, I had thought were "crabs" were only little white balls of the cotton padding which had somehow escaped from the lining of the garment. I felt pretty stupid. I also thought: "Oh my God. What will Travis do when he goes to the rooming house and finds me gone?'

It wasn't too much later that he arrived on the doorstep. Fortunately, he knew where my grand-mother lived, and the landlady at the rooming house had heard me say "Grand-ma" to the taxi driver. He looked a bit shaken, but relieved to find me.

"Why didn't you wait for me to come for you?" he asked. "The landlady said: 'She cry like a baby and run away!'"

Again, I felt embarrassed at my own lack of worldliness.

Travis came out to the back room with me then. Grand-ma seemed to know we wanted to be alone for a while. It was good not to have strangers' eyes watching our every movement. I told him, then, that I had panicked because I thought I had "the crabs", and why. We both laughed, and he hugged me and said he loved me, which I really needed at that moment.

He stayed with Grand-ma and me all that afternoon, and we bought fish and chips for tea. I had spent £6.10.0 on two nights accommodation, which should have been 2 weeks board at that time. We discussed this with Grand-ma, over the fish and chips, to decide how much board I should pay her, as she was only a pensioner. I had been saving for some time to come to Brisbane, so I had some money in reserve. But my next step had to be to find a job to pay my way.

Later, in the back room, as Travis was saying goodnight to me, he explained how he would have to catch up on his studies over the next week, and had football practice on two nights. In addition, it was his brother's turn to have the car for the week, so it would be difficult for him to get out to see me, as I was now so far away. But before he left he told me he felt better about leaving me, because I looked happier now that I was with blood, who seemed to care about me, instead of strangers. He would see me on Saturday, to take me to the football, and spend as much of Saturday night as he could with me. We exchanged long lingering kisses before we parted, feeling more comfortable in our new-found privacy than we had since my arrival in Brisbane.

That night, with the warmth of his lips still on mine, I slept soundly for the first time in 3 days, as I am about to do now.

Cetress dressed for the races in Brisbane, circa 1997.

Sylvia, on her wedding day, with Cynthia as bridesmaid and Gail Smith as flower-girl.

Sylvia, with Tom and Cetress on their 60th Wedding Anniversary, October 1993.

Sylvia on her wedding day.

Sylvia and family, with Tom and Cetress on their 60th Wedding Anniversary.

Sylvia's three sons (from left) Allan, Jason and Cameron, with Tom and Cetress at the Callide Dam.

Sylvia's grand-daughter, Carla.

A Different World

As I prepare for bed tonight I have the T.V. in my bedroom on for company, and for the late night news. There is a big football game on, between the Brisbane Broncos and some team from New South Wales. I'm not much interested in football, but there seems to be a big crowd there, and every now and then I can hear the neighbours yell out with excitement as the home team apparently makes a score. Also, having it on makes me feel closer to Travis, although he is a long way away, because I know he will be watching it too. He has always loved his football.

When we met he was playing Rugby for the University, and, later for Queensland. I remember quite vividly the first game he took me to after I moved to Brisbane. He picked me up from Grand-ma's in the car, which he had the use of that weekend, and we travelled to the Normanby Oval, where most of the club Rugby games were played in those days.

Before he arrived I couldn't wait for him to call for me. It had been several days since I saw him, and our only communication had been by telephone. This was so different from when he had been home on holidays, when we saw each other constantly. He would take over his mother's shifts at the Dairy Queen shop in order to spend time with me. We would sneak kisses behind the ice-cream machine when there were no customers in the shop. On a couple of occasions, when he was cleaning out the refrigerator at the back of the shop counter, I couldn't resist the temptation to pull him over on the floor and give him a big kiss out of the view of passers-by, after which we would both emerge laughing and looking guiltily around to make sure we hadn't been spotted.

But now, in Brisbane, things were different. I suppose it was a case of getting back to reality. At first I didn't appreciate all he had to cram into a week, what with lectures, study, assignments, football practice, games of football and visits to see me, which were now quite a journey, particularly on occasions when he didn't have the car. He was also soon to take a casual job on Saturday mornings to try to get a little extra spending money, as I still hadn't been able to get a job, but was living off my savings.

Getting back to that first football game: I'll never forget the feeling of self-consciousness I experienced as I walked with Travis into the football ground and joined a group of young University students, male and female, who all looked so different from me, in the way they stood, and the way they dressed. I looked down at my clothes, which suddenly seemed out of fashion, and the way they all talked so confidently about things that meant nothing to me, made me feel very out of place. What I wouldn't have done, at that moment, for the moral support of a couple of my country friends.

Travis introduced me to a few of the group, who were friendly enough, but I dreaded the moment, which came all too soon, when he would go off to get ready for the game. After a quick kiss, and a "wish me luck" he was gone, and there I was, all alone, like a fish out of water, amongst these people who seemed to me to come from a different planet.

After sitting there like a statue for quite a while, I thought an opportunity came for me to contribute something to the conversation, when one of the group mentioned something about a thesis.

"Oh yes" I chimed in "We have Thiess's where I come from too. My brother-in-law drives trucks for them."

That gem was greeted with a puzzled stare and a stony silence. I realized I had said something wrong, and was so embarrassed. I wished I could slide through the gap between the rows of seats and hide under the grandstand until the game was over, but there was no escape.

Fortunately, the game started almost immediately, and my faux pas was quickly forgotten by the football enthusiasts, who fell to barracking in earnest. This was another language and culture which was foreign to me.

"C'arn the 'Varsity" they cried, and "Up the Red Heavies". "Red, Red, Red" they chanted.

"Where the hell am I?" I thought.

After the game had been going for about 10 minutes, and play had ebbed and flowed, from one end of the field to the other and back again, several times, I turned to the girl next to me and said: "Which end is ours?" That, too, was greeted with raised eyebrows, and a meaningful look at the person next to her, as she pointed silently to the left. Again, I just wanted to get out of there, but I had to wait for Travis, so I was glued to the spot.

That game seemed to go on forever but at last it was over. I had no idea who had won, or what the score was. It was followed by a general milling about on the field of players and spectators, exchanging congratulations and commiserations, before the players, including Travis, eventually trooped off to shower and change before heading home. On the way home, Travis asked me how I enjoyed the game, and how I had got on with his friends. I was fairly non-committal in my replies, but as he was concentrating on the traffic and pretty worn out, he didn't probe too much at that stage. But when we got home to Grand-Ma's, he asked:

"What's the matter, sweetie? You've been pretty quiet all the way home, which is unusual for you. What happened?"

With that, it all came spilling out of me like an upturned jug.

"It was horrible." I replied. "I now know what those two travellers meant. They were right about us being from two different worlds. I couldn't understand what they were talking about, and they couldn't understand me. They think I'm stupid and must think I'm blind. I saw the looks they gave each other when I tried to join in the conversation about Thiess Brothers."

"What about Thiess Brothers?' he asked.

"One of the girls said something about writing to Thiess's, and I thought I would join in the conversation and said we had Thiess's in my town too, and Geoff worked for them."

He laughed then, and explained that the girl must have been talking about writing her thesis, and he explained what that meant.

"Stupid, stupid, stupid" I said, hitting my forehead over and over with the palm of my hand.

With that, he grabbed me and hugged and kissed me, saying: "You're not stupid. It's just all new to you. You'll get used to it, honey. You'll learn. It just takes time."

I responded by squeezing him as tightly as I could, only to have him wince, and say "Not quite so tight love, I've got a bloody sore rib there. I copped a boot in a ruck." "Oh God", I thought, "this football is not going to be my favourite thing in life. Why do they play the silly game if they get kicked in the ribs?" But at the same time I vowed that from then on I would learn a new word every week, and join a library, which I did. Next day, while job hunting, I bought a pocket dictionary which I carried with me for ages after that. I found I had plenty of time at night to read and look up, in my dictionary, new words, which I came across. I didn't see much of Travis, during the week, as his plate was pretty full, and with no T.V. then, Grand-ma tended to go to bed with the crows.

Television had only just come to Queensland at that time, and very few people had a set in their homes. Grand-ma refused to even consider getting one.

"They're only for the rich", she said, "not for poor old pensioners like me. Besides, it'll just be a flash in the pan. They'll never replace the wireless. You can get plenty of different stations, and I love my serials like 'Blue Hills' and 'When a Girl Marries'. They'll never have anything like that on this new-fangled television. The bit I've seen of it in the shop windows it seems to be all ads." (When I think of it nothing much has changed in that respect over the last 40 years!)

Except for Friday and Saturday nights, there wasn't a lot of night-life in Brisbane in those days. But with the recent advent of T.V. you could walk down to the local electrical store any night of the week and find a cluster of people standing around on the footpath, with looks of wonder on their faces, watching a flickering black and white T.V. set in operation. It certainly never occurred to any of us then that in only a few short years we would be able to watch from our own living rooms as a man, dressed like Buck Rogers, stepped from a space craft onto the surface of the moon, or witness, in brilliant colour, sporting events and calamites, as they happen, from the other side of the world.

Every morning I would be up early to enjoy a hearty breakfast which Grand-ma always prepared. "Breakfast is the most important meal of the day" she always said, and it nearly always included a helping of fresh eggs which she would have collected the previous afternoon from the fowl-house which she maintained in her back-yard. "You can't beat fresh-laid eggs from your own chooks" she would say. "It's the good food I give 'em."

After breakfast, I would dress carefully before kissing Grand-ma good-bye, and setting off on my day's job-hunting. Sometimes I would pick up a paper while waiting for the bus to take me to the city, and read the "Situations Vacant" on the way in. Other times, I would just go from shop to shop, enquiring if there were any jobs on offer. Unbeknown to me, at the time, there was a "Credit Squeeze" in operation, imposed by the Federal Government of the day, which made it harder to get a job than it had been for many years in Australia, although fortunately unemployment had not reached anything like the levels we have seen here over recent years.

Never-the-less I often had to queue for hours to try for any job which had been advertised in the paper, such as an usherette at a picture theatre or a shop assistant at Allan and Stark's (later taken over by Myers) or Weedman's. When I stood in those lines waiting for an interview I often felt despondent because, when I compared myself with the city girls, who seemed so worldly, I thought I might as well have had "BUSHIE" stamped across my forehead in large capital letters.

If I did manage to get through to a job interview, I was often given a cold stare, as if to say "What makes you think you'd be suitable for this job", or I was told "Come back when you've got some experience." I know how the young job-seekers must feel today, when confronted with the same attitude, and they know that there are thousands of others out there competing with them for the few jobs that are available.

Fairly early in the piece, I gave up any idea of getting a job in hairdressing, because I didn't feel confident with the new techniques which had been introduced during the period since Mum sold her shop, and because I felt there would be a more demanding standard in the city.

I remember one afternoon, after a long day of foot-slogging from door to door with no success, Grand-ma asked me when I got home: "Are you sure you're looking for a job, and not just going to the movies?"

With that, I burst into tears, and showed her the mass of blisters on my feet. That evoked a sympathetic response and a basin of warm disinfected water to bathe my aching feet. But my tears must have motivated her to write to Mum and Dad, because not long after that I received a letter from them begging me to come home. I wasn't ready to quit yet, and seeing Travis every weekend kept me going.

As luck would have it, the very next week I saw an advertisement for a position at Mathers Shoes, in the City, and I lined up again, with little expectation of success. This time, however, the interview was much less stressful than usual. The manageress, who conducted the interview, had such a warm, pleasant way about her, that she made me feel totally at ease, and able to present myself without any of the self-consciousness which had inhibited me at previous interviews. When at last she said: "Could you start tomorrow?" I could not believe my ears. I said: "Do you mean I've got the job?" She said: "Yes. When can you start." I said: "Tomorrow would be fine. Thank you."

I walked out feeling elated, and I couldn't wait to get home to tell Grand-ma the good news, and for Travis to telephone that night to share it with him. As a matter of fact, the lady who had conducted the interview had been so kind and pleasant to me that, even if she had turned me down, I would have walked out feeling good about myself and ready to tackle the next interview. Fortunately, that was not necessary.

Next morning I was up early and dressed for my first day at work in the big city, feeling happy that, for a change, I had a job to go to instead of searching for one. When I arrived there, after the usual introductions and being given my name-tag, one of the seniors was assigned to show me the ropes, and the first thing I had to learn about was the stock. The entire surface of the four walls of the shop itself, which was quite large, and of several back rooms, was lined from floor to ceiling with boxes upon boxes of shoes. There were several different brands and each brand had dozens of styles, each with its own name, whilst each style had many fractional fittings. As the senior girl explained it all quickly to me, I thought: "God, I'll never remember all this. They all look the same."

Then I was shown how to measure the customer's foot for the correct fractional fitting, and told that I would be responsible for keeping in order quite a large section of stock on one wall of the shop. Although I found all this fairly daunting, it also felt good to be amongst people with whom I could communicate.

The morning passed quickly, and I soon found myself in the tea room, where I was surrounded by dozens of my fellow shop assistants, both male and female, with everyone chattering away, and many smoking (as we did in those days) whilst we enjoyed the morning-tea break. The other girls were quite pleasant, and chatty, but I didn't feel confident enough to join in much at that stage. I was one of several new girls who started that day, so I didn't feel too isolated, and we tended to offer each other support. We all wondered, in one way or another, how we would ever grasp it all, but one of the older hands reassured us by saying: "Don't worry. We all felt the same when we started. It's amazing how quickly it all falls into place."

Later that week, Travis, his brother and a friend called in during the day to check out the place. No sooner had they left than I was besieged by a group of young girls, who buzzed around me like bees around a honey pot, asking excitedly: "Who were those good sorts? How do you know them?"

I replied "The best looking one is my boy-friend, the tall dark one is his brother, and the other one is a friend of theirs." Feeling a little smug at the attention which my visitors had created, I added "There's plenty more where they came from, girls."

From that moment I was "in". I was now part of the crowd, chatting away and giggling with the rest of them in the lunch room. And so I settled into the routine of work, and began, for the first time to feel almost at home in the city!

As the weeks passed, and as I became more and more accustomed to working in the city, I began thinking it might be time for me to leave Grand-ma's and strike out on my own. I was also keen to try to find accommodation which was closer both to the University and to my work. One particular event which again brought home to me how inconvenient it was for Travis with me living at my Grand-mother's place, was when he suffered a sprained ankle playing football, and he had to hobble out to see me on the bus, all the way from St Lucia to Carina, and then hitch-hike home again in the early hours of the morning long after the buses had stopped running.

One day on the way to work I called into a Real Estate Agent's office to make a tentative enquiry about renting a flatette for myself. From the reaction I got you would think I had asked for the crown jewels.

"No girlie" I was told. "Our landlords don't let flatettes to young single girls. They're only trouble. Before you know it, they're entertaining their boy-friends there, and the place gets a bad name."

I walked out feeling like a criminal. How times have changed! That same attitude today would see him on the end of an anti-discrimination suit, but in those days they got away with murder.

Not long after that, when I was having dinner with Gran, she said: "I suppose Travis is taking you out on Saturday night, as usual?"

"Yes, Gran. Why?" I asked.

"I met a nice old man the other day when I went to collect me pension. He was waiting for his too, and we got talking. We had a real nice long chat. It was good to have someone to talk to who remembers the horse and buggy days, like me, and has had some of the hardships I've had." As I write this it occurs to me that when we are young, we like to talk about what we're going to do tomorrow, always looking ahead with enthusiasm, but as we get older, we prefer to reminisce about what it was like to be young, and how everything has changed for the worse. "I've invited the gentleman out for tea on Saturday night", Gran continued, "and I'd feel a bit uncomfortable with you young ones about, and wouldn't be able to talk freely with him."

"Don't worry, Gran" I replied. "I'll be out of your hair. Speaking of which, would you like me to give you a home perm before Saturday night, so you'll look your best and be able to woo him?"

"That'd be nice" she said, with a laugh. "I've bought a new dress" (which she proceeded to show me proudly). She was clearly excited at the prospect of her first date for many years.

The next day I bought a home perm kit at the chemist in my lunch hour, and later in the week did Gran's hair with it.

Next morning, to my discomfort and Grand-ma's horror, she presented a head full of frizzy curls poking out in all directions.

"What have you done to my hair?" she demanded angrily. "It's ruined. How can I show my face on Sat'dee night looking like this?"

Gran did look such a fright, that I had this almost overpowering urge to laugh, but I managed with difficulty to suppress it and said: "Don't panic, Gran. I think its only because I couldn't set it before you went to bed. Remember you said you couldn't sleep with curlers in your hair? I'll put some in now, before I go to work, and it will look great when I comb it up tonight, you wait and see."

I proceeded to put her hair up in curlers, and all day was hoping against hope that what I had said would prove to be right. Before I got home that night, all my work-mates had heard about it in the lunch room and were amused at the story of Gran's romance and how I had possibly ruined it by frizzing her hair. As I left to go home to face the music, they all wished me luck and some jokingly offered me their spare bed if Gran kicked me out that night.

Fortunately, when I got home, Gran had already taken the curlers out and brushed her hair, and it was looking lovely. She was as pleased as I was relieved.

"You were right, dear" she said "All it needed was a good set. I feel ten years younger. He mightn't recognize me."

Within a couple of weeks Gran's romance was flourishing, and she even started talking about her boy-friend moving in "Just for the company, mind" she said. "None of that other business, I'm too old for that. I don't mind a cuddle though, and it's good to have someone my own age to talk to."

As I could see that she was a bit edgy about having him move in while I was there, I grasped this opportunity to look for a place for myself. I soon found a convenient and pleasant rooming house (private bedroom, share kitchen and bath facilities) at West End, which was much closer to my work, and also much easier for Travis to get to from the University, via the ferry. The residents were both male and female, mostly about my age, and the rules were similar to those I had experienced before, but I was now more accustomed to communicating with city people, and the atmosphere was more relaxed and friendly (possibly because I was more relaxed and friendly!)

When I told Gran I was moving out, she seemed to welcome the news, but still seemed to be a bit worried about my welfare. Before I left, we kissed and hugged, and had a few tears, but we both knew it was time to move on into a new chapter of our lives. Within days of my leaving, her gentleman friend moved into her home, and she took on a new lease of life. Although he did not live all that long after that, it is gratifying that she was able to enjoy that brief period of happiness in her twighlight years before her own health began to fail.

Thinking about how happy Grand-ma was when her boy-friend moved in brings me to thinking about how Travis and I came to share our lives on a more permanent basis, but that story will have to wait until tomorrow night.

Tom and Cetress at their 60th wedding anniversary.

Down by the Riverside

As I take up my pen and paper to begin writing tonight I glance at my left hand and notice that I don't have my engagement ring on. In a panic, I jump out of bed and hurry to the kitchen to look for it. I often take it off to wash up the dishes and clean around the sink, and usually put it on the window-sill above the sink when I do this. But I still have this feeling of panic when I realize I haven't put it back on, because as I am getting older I find I am inclined to move things and then forget where I have put them. It is therefore with a feeling of some relief that I immediately find it on the window-sill, where I left it, and I quickly slip in on again. I would hate to lose it, because it is a constant reminder of a very special, happy time in my life. As I look at it now, those happy memories come flooding back.

Not long after I had settled into the boarding house at West End, I was in bed early one night during the week reading a book. The book was "Cell 2455 Death Row", a best-seller at the time, written by Caryl Chessman, who had been convicted in the United States of a series of murders of young lovers whom he had allegedly attacked whilst they were "necking" in parked cars in "lovers' lane" type surroundings. He had been on death row, awaiting execution, for many years, whilst pursuing avenues of appeal, and had written the book protesting his innocence during that period. My reading was interrupted by an announcement, over the loud-speaker system, that there was a visitor to see me in the visitors' lounge, downstairs. Although I was not expecting a visit from Travis that evening, I was sure it would be he, so I jumped out of my bed and rushed down to see him, after throwing a house-coat over my nightie.

Sure enough, it was he. Unexpectedly, his brother had delivered the car to him that evening, and he had decided to pay me a surprise visit. I was overjoyed. In search of some privacy, we decided to go for a drive, and soon found ourselves parked near the river bank, indulging in some heavy necking. Although I couldn't wait to fall into his arms, I did have a vague uneasy feeling in the back of my mind as we parked in this dark, isolated spot, because of what I had been reading so recently in Caryl Chessman's book. However, I was soon lost in the passion of the moment, and the fear receded into my sub-conscious.

It came flooding back, in an instant, however, when I became suddenly aware of a bright light being shone into the car and the silhouette of a man appeared in the window beside me. I let out a blood-curdling scream and Travis sat bolt upright, suddenly drained of every emotion except fear, and yelled: "What? Who's there?" I screamed again and again, as visions of the "lovers' lane murders" filled my head. The silhouette in the window (which thankfully turned out to be the head of a policeman on patrol) withdrew sharply and with a loud curse, as he apparently hit his head on the roof of the car in response to my screams.

"Quieten down lady, it's the police" he said. I was so relieved I could have kissed him, but he continued.

"What do you think you're doing here? This is a public place."

"Just cuddling", Travis replied.

"Haven't you got a home to go to?" he asked.

"No" we both replied in unison.

"Well that's too bad," he said. "Move on, or I'll take you down to the police station."

We departed then, as quickly and with as much dignity as we could muster, feeling both relieved and frustrated. On the drive back to the boarding house, I said to Travis: "God that policeman gave me a fright. I thought for an instant he was the lovers' lane murderer, Caryl

Chessman on the rampage. I was relieved when I realized it was just a copper."

I then started giggling, as I pictured myself being dragged into the police station in my nightie and dressing gown, with pink fluffy slippers. But then the humour quickly vanished, as I thought more about our predicament.

"What's the matter with everyone? Haven't they ever been in love? Don't they know what it's like to want to be with someone all the time? You'd think it was a sin, the way it's banned everywhere. Can't we move in together somewhere? It would save us from being chased from pillar to post, and all the time we spend travelling to be with each other we could just spend together." I urged.

"No, sweetie", he replied. "No one would rent us a flat together unless we were married." Then, after a brief pause, he continued. "Why don't we get married?"

"Really and truly?" I asked excitedly.

"Why not," he replied. "The more I think about it, the more sense it makes. We could be together, most of the time, which is what we both want, and think of all the travelling time and money we would save."

"But what about your study?" I asked.

"Well, if we were together, a lot of the time I now spend travelling to see you, I could spend studying. And I finish my fourth year this year, which means that I could do the final 2 years part-time, as most people do. I could get a day job, and go to lectures in the evenings. All the lectures in fifth and sixth years are at night anyway, to cater for those who do articles."

As we continued this discussion, we both became more and more excited at the prospect. At one point, however, I interjected. "But what about your football? How will you manage that, what with work and study?'

"I had more or less decided I would have to give it up at the end of this season, anyway" he replied. "It's becoming too demanding of my time, besides which, my eyesight isn't what it used to be. I noticed the other night I couldn't see the ball properly under the lights, and I dropped a sitter. The guys ribbed me about it, and started calling me 'Blindenmayer'. Although they were only kidding, there was an element of truth in it because I've noticed my eyesight getting steadily worse every day. I'm sure I need new glasses."

Just then we drove past a little corner shop which was still open. "What about an ice-cream to give us food for thought while we work out the details?" said Travis, to which I readily agreed. Then, as we sat in the car outside that little shop, eating our ice-creams, we began to put some flesh on the bones of the idea, which we had so eagerly adopted.

"When do you think would be the best time for us to get married?" I asked.

"Well" said Travis, "I get a three month vacation at the end of the year, which would give us plenty of time to get married, find a place to live, and for me to get a job. Maybe you could get a couple of weeks off at that time?"

"That sounds great. I'm sure my boss will give me some time off. She's a good sport. If necessary I can make up the time later." I said. "It'll be in Biloela, where we met, of course, because both our parents are there, and it'll be easier for them to organize it there," I added.

"We'd best make it as early as possible in the long vacation so I'll have the maximum time to arrange accommodation and employment before Uni starts again next year" said Travis.

"What say we get engaged on my 21st birthday, next month" he suggested. "I haven't got any money for a ring, but no doubt Mum and Dad are planing to give me something special for my birthday, and I can't think of anything more special than enough money to buy you an engagement ring."

With that, I lifted my head and gave him a long, lingering kiss of confirmation, which I felt had a new depth of feeling and commitment to it. I know he felt it too, as his hug seemed more tender and secure at that moment than had our recent urgent, almost desperate embraces.

After a long moment, I drew back slightly and said: "You'd better take me home now. I've come out without my key, and we'll be in strife if I have to wake the landlady to get in. But just think, in a few short months we won't have to put up with this constant parting anymore."

And so we parted, less painfully than usual, and I floated up the stairs to spend an almost sleepless night in my room just bursting to tell the world about it.

Next day, while I was still floating on cloud nine, I received a letter from Mum to say that she and Dad would be down in Brisbane in a couple of weeks, as Dad had to see a specialist about his back, which had been troubling him for some time. It seems that the heavy farm work had re-activated a condition which was the result of his youthful accident, about which I have written previously. However, one of the conditions of the land ballot which he had won was that he had to hold the land for a minimum period which had not yet elapsed. In order to be able to sell the farm, which they now wished to do, and had been advised by the local doctor to do, he would need an orthopaedic specialist to certify that his spinal condition precluded him from continuing to work the farm.

I was excited by this news, because it meant I could now share my happiness about my engagement with them in person. Besides, I had missed my Mum, and it would be good to see her.

During the following week, Travis told me had had spoken to his parents on the telephone about his 21st birthday, and that when they asked him what he wanted he said: "An engagement ring for Cindy." He said that was greeted with a startled silence, before they eventually agreed, he felt not without some misgivings. To every obstacle they raised, he had an answer. This was our first inkling that our plans, which to us seemed so right and clear, may not be greeted as enthusiastically by our parents. I now realize that what the young often see as the clear road ahead, without obstacles, to their ideal goal, older people perceive as full of risks and hazards to be avoided, or at least negotiated with great care. Thankfully, the young are usually sufficiently impetuous and courageous not to be too easily diverted from their course by their parents' misgivings. Such was the case with us.

Within a few days, Travis received his birthday gift from his parents, in the form of a cheque for £50. In the meantime, one of his mates at college (who later became our best man) had introduced him to a friend whose father owned a jewellery shop, and who agreed to sell him an engagement ring at near cost price. Unbeknown to me, he and his friend picked out the ring, completed the purchase, and descended upon me at work, unexpectedly, to show it to me.

I was busy serving a customer, and looked up to see these two grinning at me like Cheshire cats. When I went over to them, they whispered, together: "We've got it."

"What?" I replied. "The engagement ring?"

"Yes" said Travis.

"Quick, quick, let me see it" I urged.

"Not yet" said Travis, teasingly. "You have to wait until I get your father's permission and then I can ask you properly."

"No" I said. "I want to see it now, please, you know it doesn't matter what Dad says, or anyone else. We're getting married. Let me see it now, please?"

"O.K." he relented, "but you can't put it on yet," and he produced what, to my eyes, was the most beautiful ring ever made, because it was a symbol of our commitment to be together.

I was bursting to put it on and show everyone, but it was still a couple of days before Mum and Dad were due to arrive, and those days seemed to pass so slowly, I thought they would never come. But at last they did.

They landed at Grandma's house on the following Saturday, and I received a phone call at the boarding house to inform me of their arrival. Travis was already on his way to pick me up to go to meet them When he arrived and I said they were already in Brisbane, he seemed to become uncharacteristically nervous.

"What's the matter," I asked. "You're not nervous are you?"

"The hell I'm not" he replied. "It's not every day I ask a father for his daughter's hand, and you've told me some pretty hair-raising stories about your father. I bet the first question he asks is 'Have you got my daughter pregnant', and the second will be 'How are you going to support her.' I know the answer to the first, but not the second. I'm not sure he will like hearing that you might have to support me for a while."

"Don't worry, it'll be alright. I might say I'm pregnant, just to see what happens."

"Like bloody hell you will. I want to get off to a good start with him, not a bad one," said Travis.

When we got to Grandma's house, there was much excitement, with hugs and kisses all round, and us all talking at once. Mum and Dad were full of questions about my job and how I had adjusted to city life, whilst I was keen to catch up on all the family news from them. Travis, however, was on tenterhooks, awaiting the opportunity to raise the subject of our engagement, keen to get the inevitable barrage of questions over as quickly as possible. When at last the initial excitement abated and we had all settled around the kitchen table enjoying a cup of tea, Travis nervously cleared his throat, and launched into it.

"Tom," he said, "Cindy and I have decided we would like to get married at the end of the year, and we would like your approval, and yours too Cetress."

Dad's reply was not quite what he expected. He said: "Well, if that's what Cynthia has decided she wants to do, no doubt she'll do it, whether I approve or not. You'll soon find out, what it's taken me 21 years to find out, namely that she has a mind of her own, and usually does what she wants. She's just like her mother in that respect."

With that Mum cut in: "What do you mean, just like her mother? If there's anyone in this family with a mind of their own, its you. She's just like her father."

Travis seemed to welcome this slight diversion into a spousal dispute, which took Mum and Dad's attention away from him. But he didn't escape entirely unscathed, and eventually father did ask the inevitable questions about how we would manage and what our plans were. But in the end they seemed reasonably satisfied with our answers. At last Dad said: "Well, life won't be easy for a while, but we started with a lot less. We had only a tent in the scrub to call home, and lived on corn beef and damper. As long as you love each other, have good health and plenty of determination, you'll make it."

"Have you got an engagement ring yet?" said Mum.

"Oh yes" I replied. "I've been dying to wear it. Quick, Travis, lets put it on now."

With that, Travis produced the ring from his pocket, slipped it on my finger, and we sealed our engagement with a kiss, before Mum and Grandma 'oohed' and 'ahed' over it, whilst Dad and Travis went out on the back verandah for a quiet beer. And so our engagement was "announced".

With that thought, I look again at the ring on my finger which I have worn now for nearly 40 years. It still gives me a warm glow of contentment to look at it with the memory of that day when Travis lovingly slipped it onto my finger for the very first time. That feeling is a pleasant introduction to a restful night's sleep, into which I now slip.

Passing the Baton

Another day has gone, and I am back in bed with my pen and paper at the ready. I realize that I will have to bring my nightly scribblings to an end soon, as Travis will be home, at last, in a couple of days. Whilst I have enjoyed meandering through my selected memories, and the process has helped me cope with the loneliness of these last weeks, his return will put an end to my need for distraction from the fears created by these lonely nights.

I went for a walk today down by the creek, where I enjoyed the peacefulness of a beautiful afternoon in those pleasant surroundings. I always enjoy looking at the creek, and watching the ducks swim in and out of the shadows cast by the trees as the sun dips towards the western horizon. As I walked, I saw a small boy skipping stones across the creek, and laughing as he managed to make one skip several times before it disappeared with a "plop" into the stream. That reminded me of my writings, because I realize I have only skipped across my life, touching just a few of my many memories, mostly the better ones. I guess that if I had been so inclined I could have written just as much about the rough patches, which we all experience and which give a balance to our lives. However, that was not the way my thoughts led me, and besides, it is only the experience of the rougher patches which makes you appreciate and cherish the happier times. Before the "stone" of my story plops finally into the creek of life, I have a few more skips to make.

Our wedding in the little church of the country town, Biloela, which had been my home for so long, was everything I had hoped it would be. I was driven to the church in Travis's father's black Customline sedan, in which we had kissed so passionately on our first real date, not that long before. It marked both a beginning of my new life, with Travis, in the city, and the end of my old life, with my parents, in the country. Both Travis and I were full of confidence about the future, heedless of the fact that we owned practically nothing, only I had a job to go back to, and Travis had borrowed £70 on the security of his life insurance policy to kick-start our married life! As we floated down the aisle and, later, away from our reception, into our life together, we wondered why our parents were so concerned about our future, when we could see no obstacles ahead which we would be unable to clear at a single bound. I often wish I could have bottled some of that youthful confidence and enthusiasm, so that I could have taken a dose of it from time to time, instead of a tablespoon from my worry bottle, when dealing with my children's problems later in my life. But I guess that is just part of life's relay.

We returned to Brisbane straight after the wedding, where we had selected a small furnished flat at West End. It took us only a few nights to become used to the fact that it was directly across the road from a heavy transport depot, where the trucks regularly started up with such a roar in the middle of the night that we first thought they must be in the next flat! It was so wonderful to have Travis beside me all night every night that I could have slept through an earthquake. I was in seventh heaven, putting minor decorating touches to our modest little home, and experimenting with new recipes to feed my man every evening. At that moment, I wanted nothing more in life.

Travis soon obtained a job at the Public Curator's Office, in the city, and I continued to work at Mathers. Travis attended lectures in the early evenings, and often studied late into the night. Still, we were together. At the end of that year, Travis passed his exams with flying colours, much to the relief of his parents. Soon after, he was offered a position as a Supreme Court Judge's Associate for his final year at University, and we were ecstatic at the prospect. It paid a whole £25 per week (which was nearly as much as the two of us had been earning from both our jobs the year before). We decided that with such a handsome wage coming in, we could soon start a family, and we started planning in that direction.

In the meantime, Mum and Dad had sold their farm and started on their next project, which was a caravan park at Yeppoon, in Central Queensland. Dad always enjoyed the challenge of a new adventure, and relished building something new from scratch, but once it was up and running, he would get the urge to sell, and move on to something new. Mum has often said that if only they had hung onto something they had built, they would have ended up as millionaires, but those who bought their projects usually ended up with the "big bucks". That proved to be the case with this project also, and no sooner was the caravan park in operation, than father sold it for a song, and moved on to buy the freehold of a pub at Westwood, west of Rockhampton.

Before we knew it, exam time was around again for Travis. He passed his final exams at the end of 1962, and we immediately began to think about his going into business on his own, as a Barrister, which he had always said he wanted to be. Both of our parents suggested that we should wait for a while, and that he would be better off staying where he was for another year or so, as it was an assured income, and there was no certainty of income from the Bar. When Mum said that was what she and Dad thought, I said: "Fancy you and Dad talking. You were always ready to take a chance. Why should I be any different. Besides, the Bar has always been Travis's goal. If he doesn't do it now, he might never do it."

So we charged ahead. The capital cost was small. An office desk, a swivel chair, two visitor's chairs, and a small book-case, all from a second-hand shop, were all that was required. He already had a few law books, and, apart from his Barrister's wig and robes, his only other acquisition at that time was an Australian Legal Digest. He and another young Barrister rented very small chambers which they shared in an old, shabby building, in Queen Street. For quite a while the briefs were few and far between, but as I had carefully saved from our wages over the last couple of years, with this goal in mind, we were ready for it, and were able to get by.

While all this was going on, I discovered I was already pregnant with my first child. When I announced the news to our parents, we threw them into another fit of worrying. It is only recently, since my children have grown up, that I have come to appreciate how they felt, and that their worrying was only out of concern for us. However, once again, like all young ones, we felt full of confidence and completely overjoyed at the prospect. Looking back, I realize that I went into pregnancy almost completely ignorant of what it involved, and how my life would change again, so dramatically, with parenthood.

When the time for my confinement drew near, Mum came down to stay with us for a while, and to be with me at the crucial time. Dad, who never liked Mum being away from him for any length of time, said: "You mollycoddle those girls too much. After all, you had your babies out in the scrub, with no one to help you [a slight exaggeration] and Cynthia will be in a modern hospital, with all the doctors, nurses and life saving equipment anyone could want." But Mum came, just the same. She wouldn't have missed it for anything.

Whilst the contrast between my child-birth and my mother's was certainly great, the contrast between the child-birth experiences of young women today and my own is just as great. I had a hard labour (over 2 days), developed toxaemia in the last days, and there was no epi-dural to manage the pain. And when I asked the sister if my husband could come into the labour ward to hold my hand, you would think I had asked for the moon.

"Oh, No, No, No" she replied. "This is no place for a husband. He would only be in the way, and would probably faint at the crucial moment. We have enough to do looking after you and your baby without having to worry about him."

Despite all the pain and effort, when my son (whom we had decided to call "Brad") did arrive, at last, I was suddenly elated as I had never been before, and felt instantly sorry for my husband that he had not been able to share this magic moment with me. Fortunately, times have changed since then. Now-a-days, if a father is not present at his child's birth, the medical staff wonder why, and he is regarded as a male chauvinist of the worst kind.

When, in the early hours of the morning, I was returned to my hospital room, and Travis and Mum were at last admitted to see me (having first been given a brief glimpse of our son through the nursery window), I was on such a high that I talked, and talked and talked, about how wonderful and beautiful our baby was. Travis agreed wholeheartedly, of course, and Mum smiled, and nodded, and said: "There is only one beautiful baby in the world, and every mother has it." Hard and all as my labour had been, I was later to learn that the birth was the easy part, and that rearing the child provides the real challenge of parenthood.

By the time Brad had started to walk, Mum and Dad had sold their Westwood Pub, and Dad had decided to go back into Real Estate business in Rockhampton. Before doing so, however, they visited Brisbane, where they stayed for a time with Grand-ma, at Carina. It was there that Dad bumped into an old mate, Jack Tobin, who operated the only Real Estate business in Carina at that time. Dad had already expressed some concerns about our living in a small flat with a toddler, and when he got talking to Jack Tobin, he enquired about houses to let. Jack said he had one at Norman Park which he thought would suit us, but it was unfurnished, and we had only a side-board and a small washing machine, which we had recently acquired on hire-purchase. But Dad generously offered to buy us the essential furniture to set up house, and so we were able to move into our first real home.

In the meantime, Travis's practice at the Bar was gradually improving. Most of his briefs were still only relatively small, but they were becoming more frequent. His earnings from his first full year in practice had amounted to only about £900, but just after we moved into the house he received his first junior brief to a silk in a large personal injury case, the fees in which were expected to run into the hundreds of pounds. It was then that we began to think about having another baby as a mate for Brad.

And so it was that I found myself pregnant for the second time, and again mother came down to be with me at the end of my term, and to care for Brad during my confinement. Then, as now, Brad seemed to enjoy having his grandmother around. They seemed to be kindred spirits even then.

When I entered the hospital on this occasion I knew better than to ask if my husband could be with me during labour. In the middle stages of my labour I recall saying to whoever would listen: "What am I doing here. After the last time I swore I'd never do it again. Yet here I am going through it all a second time. That Travis. It's all his fault. I'll never sleep with him again." But, as usual, that was all forgotten when they put Chris in my arms for the first time. He was such a cuddly, solid, little chap, my heart melted again, as it had the first time. Even today, as a grown man, he still loves his cuddles.

Following Christopher's birth, and with the steady improvement in Travis's practice, we began planning to build or buy a house of our own. Eventually, through Jack Tobin, we bought a parcel of vacant land at Camp Hill, and contracted with a builder to erect a house on it for us. It was well placed, being only a few hundred yards from the White's Hill State School, and Brad was due to start school the next year.

When our home was finished, we thought it was the most beautiful house in the world, and could not imagine how we would ever want anything better. Eventually, of course, we did, but that's another story. After moving in, we sat on the verandah, with our arms around each other, champagne glasses in hand, feeling as if we owned the world, and toasted each other's health and happiness, and that of our children asleep in their very own bedrooms. With the new year (1969) just around the corner, we justly felt some pride at our achievements from such a modest beginning only 8 years earlier.

My drooping eyelids tell me it is time to call it a night. I must finish my tale tomorrow night, as Travis will be home again the following day, and bedtime will become a time for cuddling again, instead of writing.

The Race Continues

Here I am once more, climbing into bed with pen in hand, possibly for the last time. The calendar beside my bed, upon which I have marked off each day of this separation from my husband and lover of almost 40 years, catches my eye. I feel the same sense of mounting excitement at the prospect of his return, now, as I felt all those years ago when I counted off the days between his holiday visits to the country town where we first met. We have come a long way since then, and there is so much I could write about, that it would fill a dozen more chapters, but I am determined to conclude these ramblings tonight, and so to touch only briefly upon a few events of the last 30 years, since we moved into our first home at Camp Hill in 1968. Having begun this writing, primarily for our children, so that they might gain some appreciation of their father and I as people, not just as nagging parents, and as they have shared those last 30 year with us (through both good and bad times) I do not feel the necessity to catalogue those events in the same detail as I have those of the preceding years of my life.

In the early 1970's, as my boys started, and then settled into the routine of school attendance, and associated sporting and other activities, Travis's career progressed, and became more and more demanding of his time. In the meantime, Mum and Dad had moved on to their next project, which was the establishment of a thoroughbred horse breeding stud at Bouldercombe, near Rockhampton, which they hopefully christened "Lucknow Stud". This was the culmination of a dream which father had cherished for many years. Notwithstanding his youthful accident, he had always retained his love of horses, and of racing, and had often dabbled in the ownership and training of race horses over the intervening years.

"Lucknow Stud" consisted of some 185 hectares of prime creek-front land, which father had sewn with improved pastures and fenced into paddocks of appropriate size, and upon which he constructed a large dam, irrigation system, and a set of modern stables to house his thoroughbred breeding stock, including the successful stallion, Right Formula, as principal stud sire and several well-bred brood mares. He also constructed a comfortable modern home for himself and Mum, large enough to cater for extended visits by his growing family, which by now included 6 grandchildren. Travis and I visited "Lucknow" with our children whenever we could, because the boys loved the farm, especially going swimming and fishing in the creek with their grand-mother, who had always been a keen fisherman. Their excitement as they pulled little golden perch from the creek, and cooked them to perfection, wrapped in a banana leaf and caked with mud, in the coals of an open fire under the shade of the gumtrees lining the creek-bank, or as they ran to see the ducks and geese swimming on the dam, made me appreciate the fact that Mum and Dad could provide them with this opportunity to enjoy the simple pleasures of country life which, as a youngster, I had taken for granted.

As things turned out, "Lucknow Stud" was not very aptly named, if it was predominantly good luck which my parents had anticipated it would bring them. On the contrary, ill-fortune seemed to dog them almost from the beginning of their operation of this their last business venture. Dad's first stud-sire, Right Formula, was killed accidentally in a freak fall before he had a chance to prove himself. Father then acquired two other well-bred sires to stand at his stud, namely Dusty Eyes, then aged 19, and Henry's Choice (a son of the famed King of the Tudors) which he travelled to New Zealand to acquire. Those two produced many quality off-spring over the next few years, and brought to "Lucknow Stud" a good measure of success, as well as considerable pleasure and pride to my father. However, just when all seemed to be sailing well, father's bad luck with horses reared its head again, and he lost both stallions in somewhat mysterious circumstances, within 12 months of each other. Each died suddenly, at night, in circumstances which led father to suspect sabotage (in the form of poisoning) although the official verdict of the vet in each case was "colic".

Despite these set backs, Dad and Mum soldiered on, acquiring another stallion (Galajuror) and a string of fertile, well-credentialled mares, who produced more than their fair share of winners, and enhanced the reputation of "Lucknow Stud" amongst the racing fraternity of Central Queensland, and beyond.

Through all this, Mum and Dad continued to enjoy their life, as they had always done. One of their primary forms of enjoyment was ball-room dancing. Despite his physical disabilities from his early accident, father was quite a good dancer, and Mother had always been a graceful and spirited mover on the dance floor. Together, they cut quite a fine figure. Every Saturday night, Dad would don his highly polished dancing pumps, together with his black trousers and vest, brightly coloured, embroidered shirt, and contrasting bow tie, whilst Mother would deck herself out in her finery, which consisted of one of several lavish ball gowns, complete with matching shoes and jewellery, and off they would set, with a group of friends, to the nearest pub or club where one of their favourite old-time dance bands would be playing. If there was no suitable dance being held within a reasonable distance of home they would invite their friends to "Lucknow", where they would while away the evening dancing on the timber floor of their large family room to the music of the pianola which they had acquired for just that purpose. No night of music or dancing passed without Dad pulling, from his pocket, a pair of special, well-worn dessert spoons, which he would proceed to play, like castanets, in time to the music. This was something which he had learned as a young man, and which he always enjoyed.

Meanwhile, on the home front, Travis's practice continued to flourish, and our boys were growing up in leaps and bounds. In early 1976, Travis was feeling the pressure of attempting to meet the competing demands of an ever expanding practice and his family life, which included coaching the boys football teams, attending meetings of the football club building committee and the school P & C Committee. His practice at the Bar had developed a substantial family law component, which had its own special demands, arising from the often emotional nature of the proceedings. Having reached the stage where he felt the need to limit his practice in some way, and with the imminent commencement of the new Family Law Act, he decided that the simplest and best means of doing so would be to withdraw from the family law area of practice altogether.

As fate would have it, no sooner had he made that decision and conveyed it to the solicitors who had regularly briefed him in family law matters, than I received a breathless telephone call from him at home one day.

"Are you sitting down?" he asked.

"No. Why?" I responded.

"Because I have some news which may give you a bit of a surprise." He said.

"Come on, Trav. Don't play games. Just tell me what it is" I replied, impatiently.

"Well," he said "Do you remember I told you I was going to give up family law, to limit my practice?"

"Yes," I replied, "Come on, get on with it. Just tell me!"

"I have just had the Commonwealth Attorney-General on the phone asking me to take an appointment as a Judge on the new Family Court of Australia which is being set up to administer the new Family Law Act. What do you think of that?"

"What do you think of it?" I replied.

"I'm not sure, what to think of it," he said. "Its tempting, but it's all a bit sudden, and I feel a bit young to go on the bench."

"Don't take it just because you are feeling a bit down and under pressure at the moment," I said. "Think about it for a while, and make sure before you decide. It's your decision, and whatever you decide I'll go along with."

"I haven't got too long to think about it" he replied. "He wants an answer by early next week. That really only gives me the week-end to decide. I guess we'll talk about it some more when I get home, but I thought I'd start you thinking about it right away. I'll need all the help I can get. It's not an easy choice."

Over that week-end we did a lot of talking and thinking about this new turn which life was taking, and Travis also spent a lot of time talking over the pros and cons with his father (who happened to be down from Darwin, where his parents were living at that time), with his accountant, and with one or two of his special friends. Travis was very much in two minds about it, and I kept telling him it was his decision, and that I didn't want to influence him one way or the other. In the end, he decided to accept the offer, as he felt it would be a new challenge to give impetus to his professional life at a time when he felt that his career was becoming more and more demanding but less rewarding, in an emotional sense. And so it was decided, and with the decision our life took on a new and challenging dimension.

No sooner had we made and confirmed that decision than I received a most distraught call from my mother to inform me, in rather garbled terms, that Dad had just been taken off to hospital in the ambulance having somehow broken both his legs in yet another tragic accident involving a horse. We were later to learn in more detail what had happened.

He had been doing something so simple, and so routine, that the danger inherent in it was not apparent, even to his experienced eye. He had gone down to the stables early in the morning, having seen from the back verandah of the house that 3 of his mares had somehow got out of their paddock and were roaming in the paddock adjacent to the stable where his stallion, Galajuror, was housed. When he got there, he found that someone had left open the temporary "gate" between the two paddocks. That "gate" consisted only of a galvanised iron pipe, some 4 metres long and 4 cms in diameter anchored at one end to the gate post, but free at the other end, which, when the "gate" was closed, slotted into a bracket fixed to the opposite post, but when open, was allowed simply to rest on the ground. It was in the latter position that he found it.

He soon rounded up the 3 mares, and shepherded them towards the open "gate" into their holding paddock. The first 2 went through the gate without trouble, and trotted on into their yard. The third mare, however, was more hesitant, and after passing through the gate, stopped just inside, and turned back, as if undecided. Father stepped forward, nearer to the section of the rail touching the ground, in order to usher the mare gently on into her paddock. Just as he did so, the mare made a dash for freedom, attempting to pass between him and the gate post to which the high end of the rail was attached. In doing so she cannoned into the rail, causing the free end to whip around with terrific force, catching Dad full across both shins, and smashing both his legs severely between knee and ankle.

How he lay there for what seemed like hours, in dreadful pain, crying out vainly for help, before dragging himself, inch by inch, to his car parked tantalizingly only metres away, and somehow managed to open the door and depress the horn to attract attention to his plight, is part of his story, which I shall not detail here. What he did later relate to me was how, lying there once again dreadfully injured by a horse which he loved, the feeling of complete isolation and gut-wrenching fear which he had experienced in a similar situation all those years ago came flooding back.

His legs were so badly shattered that, once again, he was forced to undergo months of painful treatment, including several operations, and hours of physiotherapy in hospital. On this occasion, instead of his mother, it was my mother who visited him daily, and encouraged him to battle on. One of the first things she did was to buy him a new pair of dancing pumps, which she placed prominently at the end of his bed for him to see. Whenever he was down, and needed encouragement to keep up the struggle towards rehabilitation, she would take hold of his hand, and gently remind him of his dancing shoes awaiting there to be filled by him, so that once again she could enjoy the first waltz of the evening with him. I have no doubt that her words of encouragement were instrumental in the recovery which he eventually made, although he was never again free of pain in his battered legs. He did, however, get to wear his dancing shoes again, although he was not quite as nimble as he once was.

As I think of Mum now, holding his hand, as he sits forlornly in the old folks home, I am conscious of the sad fact that, whilst he was able with her help and encouragement to bring all of his strength and determination to bear to overcome his physical injuries on that occasion, there is nothing he or anyone else can do to fight off the dementia which has now overtaken him.

In his declining years, two things Dad loved to do were to talk about his life story, "Walk a Mile in My Shoes", which he had written after his second accident forced him into retirement, and to play the spoons, at every opportunity. I always thought that those two things would stay with him until the day he dies. Sadly, that is not the case. When I have seen him recently in the old folks home, he displays no memory of ever having written his book, and although he made an attempt, with Mum's encouragement, to play the spoons at a recent Christmas singalong he had forgotten how to manipulate the spoons and seemed not to know what he held them for.

Those thoughts cause tears to well up in my eyes, and drop down onto the page where I am writing. They also make me feel lonely and scared again. But I am comforted then by the thought that my lover will be home tomorrow night, and that I will once again feel happy and secure as I cuddle into him and enjoy the chemistry which is between us. I make a promise to myself, then, not to dwell on the past, not to look forward too much into the future, but just to live for the present and make the most of our just being together.

Full Circle

It has been a while now since I picked up my pen for my nightly scribblings. I thought that I had finished all that, with the return home of my husband, since the need to fill the void of loneliness at bed-time disappeared with his presence. But tonight is a special night, as I sit at the table in our holiday unit in Cairns, pondering the events of a remarkable day. Tonight, my writing is inspired, not, as before, by nostalgia born of loneliness, but by sheer joy at the experience I shared with my husband and son today, as we welcomed a new life into our family circle.

We have just enjoyed the special privilege of witnessing the miracle of the birth of our first grand-child, to be named Thomas Edwin, after each of his great-grandfathers on his father's side. We feel truly privileged that Polly and Chris allowed us to share that very special time with them, as we watched, in awe, young Thomas emerge head first from his mother's birth canal and take his first wide-eyed peek at the world which he had just entered.

In the hours leading up to the birth, Travis had waited patiently outside the birthing suite of the Cairns Base Hospital, whilst Polly's mother (Ruth), Christopher, Polly's best friend (Shelley) and myself, together with young Elly (and, from time to time, the midwife) kept vigil inside the suite, encouraging and supporting Polly through her long, drug-free, ordeal. For my part, I was mainly occupied in keeping young Elly amused (between her frequent enquiries as to when her baby brother or sister would arrive) with stories, or with encouragement in respect of her colouring of a children's colouring book which Travis had brought back after one of his visits to the nearby kiosk for refreshments. As the imminent birth drew nearer, I was very pleased to hear Christopher say, in a slightly panicky voice:

"Quick, Mum. Go and get Dad before he misses out on this wonderful moment."

And what a wonderful moment it was to be! Christopher's invitation to his father to be present to share that moment somehow made up for the fact that, in keeping with the thinking of the time, Travis had not been permitted to witness the birth of our children.

I recall that as I stood there watching the last moments of Thomas' birth and the first moments of his life, I seemed to be living in 3 different time zones, all at once. Seeing Chris and Polly welcome their son into the world with joyous wonder took me instantly back to the elation which Trav and I felt at the birth of our 2 sons, all those years before. At the same time, I felt I was my mother, experiencing the birth of her grand-child. Seeing a child of my own experiencing the same feelings as my mother had witnessed me feeling, at the bringing of a new life into the world, gave me a real sense of timelessness, almost of immortality, as if I were not just me, the individual, but part of a great cycle of life and death which makes up the whole, perpetual human experience.

Soon after the birth, when young Thomas was placed in my arms for the first time, I felt such a strong surge of love for him that I could only stare in awe at his lovely little face and wonder what lay ahead for this tiny bundle of humanity. I thought how absolutely innocent his face looked at that moment, and could not help but think that it was a purity and innocence which would be eroded by the experiences of life which he would encounter over the years ahead. Hopefully, though, his parents and grand-parents will be there to guide him through, and to provide the armour of their love to protect him from, the worst of life's tribulations.

As I recall those thoughts and feelings, sadly they bring my thoughts back to my Dad. I recall how, when last I saw him in the old folks home, I noticed that his eyes, too, had that trusting, innocent look, almost of a child. That brings to me an awareness of how we humans travel the full circle of life. If we live long enough to reach old age, we tend to regress to early childhood, but, sadly, without childhood's promise of growth and development into a thinking, caring and self-reliant human being.

But, for now, I put those thoughts aside, and look forward to all the pleasures of being a grand-parent, which Travis and I will be able to share over the coming years. We have already tasted those pleasures, through our contact with the lovely Elly. Her bright, happy smile as she runs to hug and kiss us when we arrive, her breezy chatter about the every-day events of her life; her eager inclusion of us in her little childhood games; the loveliness of her interactions with her mother as she bathes and prepares for bed; the soft, sweet way she listens, attentively, to a bed-time story before drifting off into untroubled sleep; the excitement and wonder she had displayed as she witnessed Tom's miraculous birth and the gentle, loving way in which she holds and talks to him at every opportunity: these are the things which already enrich our lives, and we know that, with the birth of Thomas, a new chapter in our book of life has begun. It is a chapter to be cherished, nurtured and enjoyed to the fullest. Tonight, I will sleep peacefully in my husband's arms, knowing that when we awake tomorrow, there will be something new and exciting to enjoy and experience together: getting to know our new grand-child.

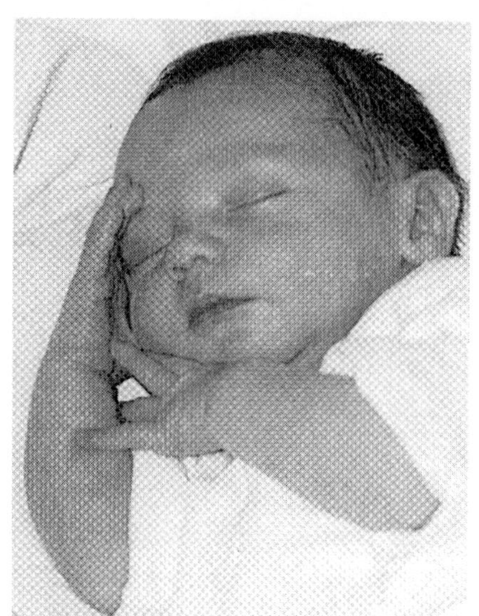

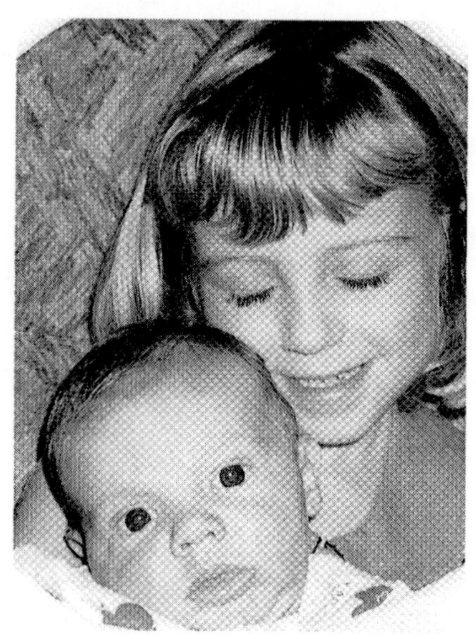

Cynthia and Travis at
Chris and Polly's wedding 1999.

The End

Epilogue

Twelve years have now passed since I wrote most of the above. Many changes have occurred in our lives in that time. First Dad, and then Mum, have passed away – Dad in September 2000, and Mum in November 2002. When your parents are alive you think of them as being indestructible. Sadly, they are not.

When Mum was alive, and I was in Brisbane, for many years I would telephone her every morning. Now, most mornings at some point I look at the 'phone and wish I could still ring her. But, instead, I now talk to her, silently, in my head. When I have to undergo a medical procedure or test of some kind, the child still comes out in me and I yearn for the emotional support of my mother. So, I carry a miniature picture of her tucked inside my bra, near my heart. That makes me feel safer and more secure that she is still looking over me.

As for Dad, I have felt his presence most strongly when I have been writing - a late-life passion that I must have inherited from him. He was very passionate about his auto-biography, Walk a Mile in My Shoes, which he published and distributed himself back in 1981. Soon after his self-published version appeared, he had approaches from publishing houses seeking to edit and re-publish it under their banners. This was quite unusual, and the reverse of the usual scenario in which authors hawk their manuscripts around the professional houses desperately, and mostly fruitlessly, looking for a publisher. But Dad steadfastly rejected these approaches, saying, "They'd only change it. No bugger's going to change a bloody word of my story!"

Despite that attitude, I am quite sure that he would now be very proud that, since the copyright of his book passed to me, it has been beautifully, and faithfully re-published (incorporating a number of his previously unpublished bush poems) by CQU Press, in 2000, re-printed by that publisher in 2008, and is now about to be republished (effectively for a fourth time) by Boolarong Press. So, his homespun literary work has survived in circulation for over 30 years, quite a remarkable achievement for a man of limited formal education. I know that he received hundreds of letters from happy readers, and that trend has continued since his death, with many such letters finding their way to me.

People have said to me, "Wouldn't it have been wonderful if Tom could have known how successful his book would become." I believe that, spiritually, he does.

Travis retired at the end of 2002, and we have bought a holiday home in Cairns, not far from Chris's and Polly's home, where we go to spend the winter months each year and enjoy the company, and share in the upbringing of our grandchildren

As I think back now, and read over what I wrote in my early chapters about Mum and Dad in their declining years, it scares me to think that we are only a few years short of the ages that they then were. We have reached the stage where we are beginning to contemplate the possibility of graduating to a retirement village with aged-care facilities, particularly when our arthritic aches and pains are at their worst, or some contemporary dies. However, we try to banish those bleak thoughts from our minds and keep as busy as we can interacting with friends and family.

Another pass-time I have embraced has been the writing of more books, in which I have tried my hand at fiction. With Travis as my not always obedient but ever helpful secretary/editor and typist, I have written and self-published Myra's Escape from the Shadows (in 2002) and Guilty Secrets (in 2008). In 2010/11, I wrote my latest (and probably my last) novel, Façades, which was published by Interactive Publications ("IP") of Brisbane. Apart from filling in much of our time and keeping our minds active, my writing hobby has had some pleasing spin-offs. One of the most enjoyable occurred when a reporting team from Channel 9's A Current Affair came to Cairns where they shot an amusing segment involving us and our son, Christopher, which aired on that programme soon after. The crew, led by Brady Halls, was such a bright, happy, friendly bunch that we enjoyed a really fun-filled day. Partly as a result of that, I also enjoyed some light-hearted radio interviews with radio personalities in both Cairns and Brisbane.

Another spin-off from the A Current Affair feature was a brief appearance by both Travis and me as extras in the filming in Cairns of an ABC adventure series to be called "The Straits", which will go to air sometime in 2012.

Although we spend about four months of each year in Cairns, mainly for the purpose of keeping in touch with Chris, Polly and their children, we also try to maintain a life of our own, so that our children's and grandchildren's lives do not become our lives. So, in addition to my writing hobby, we maintain a small circle of close friends in both Cairns and Brisbane. Our elder son, Brad, lives in Brisbane, and his presence here provides the strong incentive for us always to return here. Travis also holds a permanent casual position with a leading Cairns law firm, which he visits weekly, when we are there, and with which he communicates regularly by 'phone and over the Internet when in Brisbane.

Another important change in our lives has been the birth of a second grandson, Sam, who is a joy and a blessing. He was born just 16 months after his brother, Tom, whose amazing birth I recorded in the chapter headed "Full Circle".

Elly is now a young woman of 17 years, as beautiful in nature as she is in appearance. We have been fortunate to see our three grandchildren grow from infancy, in Elly's case into young adulthood, and in Tom's and Sam's cases, to the verge of adolescence.

Not long ago I witnessed Elly going off to a school "Prom". When I saw her, a picture of elegance in a long, backless frock, with her long blond hair beautifully coiffed, I found it an amazing, but heart-warming contrast with my memory of her as the little five-year-old I had seen standing at the foot of her mother's birthing table excitedly awaiting and then witnessing the birth of her baby brother, Tom.

Tom, who is now as tall as I, and Sam, who is not much shorter, are strong, athletic, boisterous boys, both very much into sports, especially AFL football, and cricket. On our visits to Cairns, Travis very much enjoys attending, and sometimes playing a minor supporting role in, their AFL games. He also eagerly participates in kicking a football during the frequent informal practice sessions they hold, either in the cul-de-sac street outside their home, or at one of the nearby parks or sports grounds. I recall how thrilled he was when Tom, while preparing to go to the sports ground to kick the ball with some of his friends and Sam, turned to him and asked, "Poppy. Are you coming with us for a kick?" Of course he did, and enjoyed it immensely, even though he returned home nearly exhausted after keeping up with several energetic and enthusiastic young budding Jonathan Browns or Tony Abletts.

All three of our grandchildren, not to mention Polly and Chris, are very attached to their little, black Poodle, called Molly. There was a period during Tom's earlier years at school when Molly discovered a means of escape from their house yard, and made her way to the school, where she turned up in Tom's classroom to sit at his side. On a couple of those occasions, when we were in Cairns, we received a call from Polly asking if we could pick up Molly from the school and take her to our place until she could get home from her work at the pre-school, to retrieve her. Travis reported that when he arrived at the school for that purpose, Tom appeared quite chuffed that Molly had sought him out and found him amongst the large number of children at the school, to which she had never previously been. Soon after that, Chris and Polly re-secured their yard against Molly's clever escape methods.

Molly, like so many of her breed, is an endearing, and intelligent little creature. One of her obsessions is with chasing and retrieving a tennis ball, or some other object of similar size which she will suddenly select for that purpose. She will happily engage in that recreation for hours on end if she finds a willing human partner, which Travis often becomes.

Perhaps the most remarkable change in our lives, and everyone else's, has been in the field of technology. From the massive changes in computer technology, and the growth of the Internet, through to the advent of "smart phones" that can "surf the net", take and transmit photographs, and perform a myriad of other complex functions too numerous to recite (besides making telephone calls!), to iPods and e-Readers that can store masses of information, including thousands of books, in a device so small it fits in a person's pocket or hand-bag, the world has become a place that previous generations would not comprehend.

All this technology has created wonderful advantages for commerce, and for communication around the world and within families. But, marvellous and all as these advances are, there are also some disadvantages from a purely social point of view.

We are all becoming more and more dependant, both practically and emotionally, on our devices. It sometimes appears that people have their mobile phones attached to their heads (and, indeed, some quite literally do!) as they walk the streets and shopping centres conducting animated conversations with unseen persons, while apparently oblivious to those around them. This practice has even become a health hazard, in the sense that such people ignore traffic and other road hazards at their peril while absorbed in their phone conversations.

All this obsession with and excessive dependence upon technology is quite foreign to people of my generation, who grew up through an era when radios were as big as modern small refrigerators, with batteries weighing several kilograms, and when telephones operated only from fixed locations through fixed wires, and were a rare luxury, mostly available only to the wealthy or to businesses. To my father's and mother's generation, even those rudimentary communication devices were miraculous, and I cannot imagine their response to modern technology of the types I have only briefly touched upon.

I attended a party recently, during which, while standing in groups talking, we would be frequently interrupted by the sound of someone's mobile phone ringing. The person called would immediately excuse themselves, and retreat outdoors to answer it. I don't know why it is, but it seems to me that most people talk more loudly than normal on a mobile phone, giving anyone within earshot an unwanted insight into their private business. Looking around the room from time to time, I also noticed one or two other guests sitting, talking to no one, but busily sending or receiving text messages on their phones.

Maybe I'm just an old fogey, but I do hope that future generations will not become so mesmerised by these wonderful gadgets that they lose the benefits of normal human interaction, including the enjoyment of sharing a good belly-laugh with a friend, or an old fashioned sing song, or of personally lending a sympathetic ear to someone else's problems.

Recently I had some younger people visiting me at home, during which I had occasion to be searching for something in my garage. During my searching, a plastic packet containing a bundle of Travis's old love-letters to me, fell down. I read one of the letters to my young friend, who turned excitedly to her fiancée and said, "Oh! Please write me a love-letter! Will you please write me one?" It was then I fully realised that personal letters are becoming a thing of the past, replaced by email and texting.

Thinking of all these changes, and the many more that my grandchildren will encounter during their lives, I am glad that I have my Dad's book to hand down to them and through them to their children, and their children's children, in order to preserve for them some of the personal family history experienced by my father and his generation. I hope that this little book of mine may also contribute, in a small way to that preservation.